JUNE 28/00   ALAN M

Y0-BSO-152

-0483

New Horizons
Computer Learning Centers, Inc.

PUBLISHING CENTER

Specializing in Custom PC and Macintosh Courseware

ADVANCED
Excel 2000 for Windows 95

APPROVED COURSEWARE

— *Corporate Offices* —
1231 East Dyer Road • Santa Ana, CA 92705 • (800) 864-2456

Advanced

Excel 2000

MICROSOFT OFFICE

user3
New Horizons CLC

Copyright 1985-1999 Microsoft Corporation. All rights reserved.
This program is protected by US and international copyright laws
as described in Help About.

Your Help Desk phone number is   770-234-4677

Your password for this class is   243 299 388 127

New Horizons
Computer Learning Centers, Inc.

– ACKNOWLEDGMENTS –

New Horizons Courseware Development Staff

Vice President of Courseware
Bill Baker

Courseware Development Manager
Joseph Molnar

Production Supervisor
Jason Teitel

Translation Coordinator
Mario Cortez

Administrative Assistant
Tasha Ellis

Editorial Staff
Steve Dong, Judy Ly, George Markwick,
Nancy Roux, Darren Yamasaki, Michael Sullivan

Graphics/Layout Specialists
Damon Wong, Brad Moore

Development Support
Carl Alessi, Barbara Andrews,
Keith Menor, Daniel Murphy, Bill Sullivan

"I'm certified.
Are you?"

APPROVED COURSEWARE

Prove your Microsoft Office knowledge –
get MOUS certified at
New Horizons Computer Learning Centers.

Microsoft Office User Specialist Program (MOUS) Certification is Microsoft's verification of your Microsoft Office skills. Having MOUS Certification on your resume can provide you with a higher level of opportunity in the hiring, placement, and career development process.

How to get the MOUS Certification

You can receive a MOUS certification in a single Microsoft Office Program or all five of them – Word, Excel, PowerPoint, Access and Outlook. Since the New Horizons courseware booklet you are using here contains only Microsoft Authorized Courseware Material, all you need to do is take your Microsoft Office classes at New Horizons and then pass the appropriate exams.

Exams are available at both the Core and Expert levels for each program, and once you have passed all five exams at the Expert level, you'll become a MOUS Master!

Get started now!

Contact your Account Executive about MOUS Certification today! The class you are in right now may get you on your way towards MOUS Certification. Your Account Executive can tell you how our courses fit into your MOUS certification plans.

www.newhorizons.com

Table of Contents

Illustrations

Exercise Files

EXCEL09.XLS

EXCEL10.XLS

EXCEL11.XLS

EXCEL12.XLS

Support Files

NONE

Supplemental Applications

NONE

Advanced
Excel 2000 for Windows 95
PREFACE

Computer Accounting

Excel 2000 for Windows 95/98 and
Windows NT is a powerful worksheet
program that helps you document and
manage complex numerical data.

The Software Worksheet

Throughout history, human beings have calculated, manipulated, and organized numerical information. The need for precise record keeping has always presented a challenge. Computers brought about a revolution in the speed and ease of data processing. Specialized programs called electronic worksheets alleviated many of the problems associated with modern accounting.

From small-business owners to major corporations, software worksheets became a valuable tool. Worksheet programs have become very sophisticated over the years and provide the user with more powerful features. Excel enables you to create and manage complex worksheets, and learn the program easily.

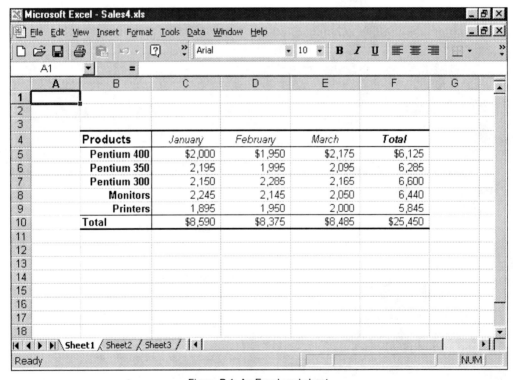

Figure P.1: An Excel worksheet

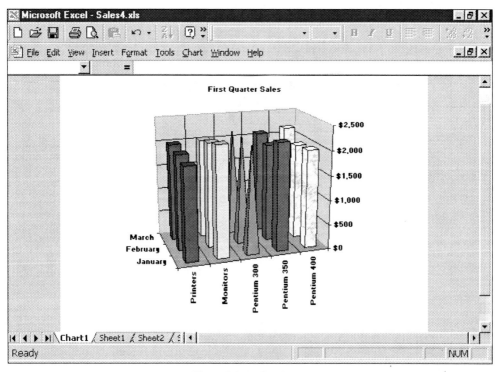

Figure P.2: An Excel chart

Overview: Excel 2000 for Windows 95

Excel 2000 is designed to operate on either the Windows 95/98 or the Windows NT platform. It is a worksheet application that allows you to organize interrelated numerical information. You can think of a worksheet program as a very sophisticated ledger. Data is entered electronically, so numerical figures can be updated without time-consuming recalculations or corrections. Since Excel 2000 is a Windows program, .the Graphical User Interface (GUI) offers an intuitive environment, allowing you to improve the appearance of the worksheet through character and numerical formatting.

Editing features enable data to be moved and copied throughout the worksheet. Excel is designed on a workbook concept; it is possible to have 255 worksheets of interrelated data under one file name.

Excel can also create charts to present your data visually. The Chart Wizard enables you to transform data into chart presentations quickly and easily. Your data can appear as a bar, line, area, XY, or pie chart. You can choose from fourteen standard chart types with seventy-three sub-types, or twenty custom types. Charts can

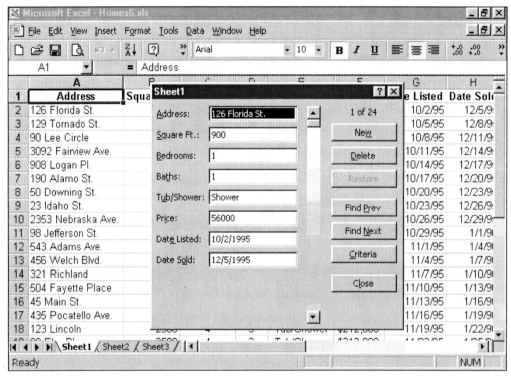

Figure P.3: An Excel database

be printed as separate documents, or as part of a worksheet. You can also use the Microsoft Map application, that comes bundled with Microsoft Office 2000, to create geographical maps from Excel worksheet data.

You can import graphics as pictures from other applications to enhance the appearance of your worksheet, and draw graphics using lines, ovals, arcs, rectangles, and text. The advanced tools of Excel allow you to manage data stored in a worksheet as if it were a database. You can query external database files created by other database applications. You can sort and extract information and view it elsewhere in the workbook. You can create cross-tabulated reports of items making up the database records, and perform advanced analysis on groups of numerical data.

The Excel window is intuitive; it anticipates the worksheet needs of the user. The toolbars, which contain the most commonly used worksheet commands and actions, are specifically designed for use with a mouse.

How to Use this Manual

Title Page

Each manual is written in modular learning blocks that introduce users to related concepts and exercises. Every module begins with a title page that identifies the start of a module and encapsulates the main concepts covered in the module.

Exercise Preview

Each exercise is preceded by an explanation of the concepts to be illustrated. Appropriate tips, tricks, and shortcuts that you may find useful are included in a list format for quick reading and referencing.

Module Preview

Each module begins with a presentation to illustrate concepts a user must understand to complete the exercises. After reading the Preview, you'll be prepared to progress to individual exercises.

Step-by-Step Exercise

Module exercises are presented in a format designed for all types of users. The left column is a step-by-step path to complete the exercise. The right column complements the exercise steps, providing additional information.

The Objectives

Module objectives are stated on a separate page. Each objective corresponds to a module exercise, identified by letters for referencing.

Module Review

Each module concludes with a brief review and practice session that reinforce and strengthen your understanding of the lessons.

Each manual enables users to assess application knowledge level.
The Pre-test appears at the end of the Preface. The Post-test appears after the last module.

Modular Learning Blocks

This manual consists of sections of related information called modules. A module is designed for two hours of instructor-led training. Modules may also be used in lab workshops and for self-study.

Each manual follows the normal class content which includes sample exercises for you to complete. The exercises contain keystroke sequences to familiarize you with the operation of the program.

By design, modules may be used independently or out of sequence. An exercise file that is used in more than one module is given a unique name for each new module.

Formatting Conventions

Introductions to exercises and the exercises are presented in the typeface Helvetica. As a further aid to users, there are two format conventions used in the step-by-step exercises.

Computer interaction with the user (such as commands, prompts, menu titles, references to text on the screen, dialog box names and options) are presented in a box to distinguish them from manual text. For example:

Press Enter.

Select the I in Introduction.

Keyboard commands are rendered in the same manner. When commands are to be issued simultaneously, a plus sign (+) separates the keystrokes. When commands are to be issued sequentially, a comma (,) separates them.

Text a user types as part of an exercise is rendered in Courier bold to simulate typewriter text:

Now is the time for all...

As a rule, the figure (screen capture) at the top of the first page of the steps of an exercise will reflect the results of having completed the steps, or at least a majority of the steps, of the exercise.

File Extensions

By default Windows 95 does not display file extensions. For the purpose of clarity this manual includes file extensions. Please refer to your Windows 95 documentation to enable the display of MS-DOS file extensions.

Copying Exercise Files

Before starting the program you will need to create a folder on your desktop. While completing the class and these exercises, you will be saving your files to this folder, which will be named TEMP.

Exercise files are also available from the New Horizons web site:

http://www.newhorizons.com/courses/materials/exercise/index.cfm

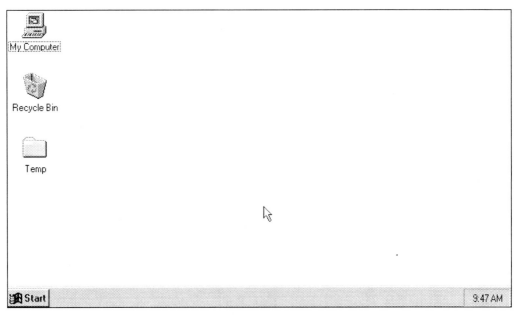

Figure P.4: The Temp folder on the desktop

Exercise: Getting Started

Step by Step	Additional Information
1. Turn on your computer.	
2. Close all open windows.	This places your computer at the desktop.
3. Right-click the desktop.	A shortcut menu opens.
4. Move the pointer to New.	The New submenu opens.
5. Click Folder.	This creates a new, untitled folder on your desktop. It is selected so you can enter the name by typing.
6. Type **Temp** Enter.	You will store all your files in this folder.
7. Place the Exercise disk in the (A:) floppy drive.	
8. Double-click the My Computer icon.	The My Computer window opens.

Step by Step	Additional Information
9. Double-click the `3½ Floppy (A:)` icon.	The 3½ Floppy (A:) window opens.
10. Press `Control` + `A`.	To select all the files.
11. Drag the selected files to the `Temp` folder.	To copy the files to the Temp folder.
12. Close all open windows.	

This courseware is based on software available in the Microsoft Office 2000 Premium Edition.

Installation Notes

The exercises in this manual were developed with a Typical Office 2000 installation.

Exercise D of Module 9 demonstrates the Analysis Toolpak which is not included in the Typical install. When you click OK in Step 5, you are advised that the feature is not installed and asked if you want to install it. Click Yes and Excel searches for the files on the installation CD-ROM. If the CD-ROM is not in the CD-ROM drive, insert it or browse to the location of the installation files and click OK to install the missing component.

Exercise E of Module 10 demonstrates the Solver feature which is not included in the Typical install. When you click OK in Step 6, you are advised that the feature is not installed and asked if you want to install it. Click Yes and Excel searches for the files on the installation CD-ROM. If the CD-ROM is not in the CD-ROM drive, insert it or browse to the location of the installation files and click OK to install the missing component.

Exercise D of Module 12 demonstrates the templates feature which is not included in the Typical install. When you click OK in Step 6, you are advised that the feature is not installed and asked if you want to install it. Click Yes and Excel searches for the files on the installation CD-ROM. If the CD-ROM is not in the CD-ROM drive, insert it or browse to the location of the installation files) and click OK to install the missing component.

Advanced Excel 2000 for Windows 95 Pre-test

Directions: Circle the correct answers

Module 9

1. An IF function formula has three arguments: the test, an "if true" statement, and an "if false" statement. (TRUE – FALSE)
2. IF functions can be nested within one another. (TRUE – FALSE)
3. The AND logical function tests multiple conditions, of which any can be true. (TRUE – FALSE)
4. IF functions cannot display text strings; they can only calculate results. (TRUE – FALSE)
5. The NOT logical function returns the reverse value for the condition tested. (TRUE – FALSE)
6. Goal Seek finds a solution by...
   a. changing the formula cell.
   b. adjusting the value in a single cell.
   c. adjusting the values in multiple cells.
   d. none of the above
7. The correct syntax for the AND function in an IF logical formula is
   a. =AND(IF(B2>10000,B8>4),B2*B4,B2*E4)
   b. =AND(=IF(B2>10000,B8>4),B2*B4,B2*E4)
   c. =IF(AND(B2>10000,B8>4),B2*B4,B2*E4)
   d. =(IF/AND((B2>10000,B8>4),B2*B4,B2*E4))

Module 10

1. If a series moves down a column, a one-variable data table should have a column input cell. (TRUE – FALSE)
2. The top row of a one-variable data table can contain text, sample formulas, or a data series. (TRUE – FALSE)
3. It is not necessary to include the left column labels in a VLOOKUP. (TRUE – FALSE)
4. The HLOOKUP function searches a row for matching items. (TRUE – FALSE)
5. A two-variable data table requires two variable cells, and both a row and column series to calculate variable results. (TRUE – FALSE)
6. For an HLOOKUP to work properly, you must include:
   a. The top row of labels or values in the data table.
   b. The left column of labels or values in the data table.
   c. Both the top row and left column of labels and values.
   d. None of the above
7. A two-variable data table must contain:
   a. A row input cell.
   b. A column input cell.
   c. Both row and column input cells.
   d. none of the above

Module 11

1. You can record function procedures. (TRUE – FALSE)
2. A function procedure requires data from the user to return a value. (TRUE – FALSE)
3. A function procedure can display a message. (TRUE – FALSE)
4. A function procedure can be written directly on a worksheet. (TRUE – FALSE)
5. Function procedures are capable of performing logical tests. (TRUE – FALSE)
6. Function procedures begin and end with the keywords...
   a. Sub and End Function.
   b. Function and End Function.
   c. Sub and End Sub.
   d. Function and End Sub.
7. Which application object statement accesses the VLOOKUP function?
   a. App.VLookup
   b. VLookup.App
   c. Application.VLookup
   d. AppVLookup

Module 12

1. Custom menus and items cannot be accessed using keystrokes. (TRUE – FALSE)
2. While the Customize dialog box is open, you can move default menus to any position on the menu bar. (TRUE – FALSE)
3. Custom toolbars do not have the characteristics of default toolbars. (TRUE – FALSE)
4. The default folder for a custom template is the Templates folder. (TRUE – FALSE)
5. Custom tools have no commands or macros assigned to them. (TRUE – FALSE)
6. The character used to denote an underlined menu letter is...
   a. *.
   b. $.
   c. &.
   d. #.
7. Which extension is the correct extension for an Excel Template?
   a. .xls
   b. .xlt
   c. .xlw
   d. .tmp

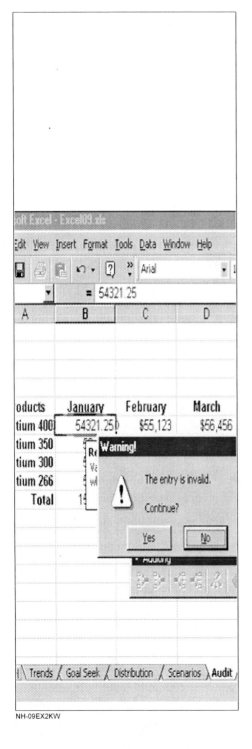

IF Logic

Excel 2000 features commands and functions that allow you to answer hypothetical questions and predict possible results.

— User Notes —

Module Preview: IF Logic

Excel can do more than just organize and calculate numbers. The program includes features that analyze data in order to predict different outcomes. This "what if" analysis is performed using the Scenario Manager, Goal Seek, trend options, and logical functions.

For example, if for the past three years, you have recorded your company's profits and losses, you can forecast a trend. A trend is a data series that follows a specific pattern. Excel allows you to calculate linear and growth series using special options. Excel's auditing feature displays relationships among cells with lines and arrows so that you can quickly determine whether you have created appropriate formulas.

Once you have predicted trends, the Scenario Manager can track various outcomes. Suppose you have predicted best- and worst-case scenarios

for the next three years. The Scenario Manager can store multiple sets of data that allow you to see instant updates of different outcomes.

Excel also employs special logical functions that test the contents in a cell or range against defined conditions before displaying a result based on the outcome of the test. For example, a function in a cell could specify that if an entered value is less than 100, it will be multiplied by 5 while a value higher than 100 will be multiplied by 3. You can also refine your tests by combining logical functions. The AND, OR, and NOT functions allow you to test multiple sets of conditions.

If you have questions that begin with "what if," then employ Excel's analytical power to find the answers. The program's ability to calculate trends, manage scenarios, and perform logical testing makes data analysis easy.

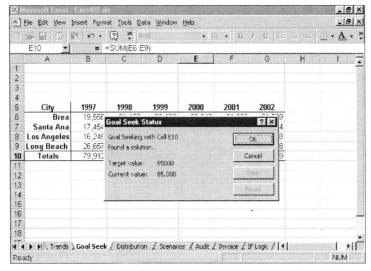

Figure 9.1: Using Goal Seek

— User Notes —

Module Objectives

Upon completion of this module,
you will master the skills necessary to:

A.   Employ Trend Analysis

B.   Use Goal Seek

C.   Determine Frequency Distribution

D.   Use Scenario Manager

E.   Audit a Worksheet

F.   Use Data Validation

G.   Nest an IF Function

H.   Combine Logical Functions

I.   Use Conditional Formatting

Before You Begin Exercise A

Employ Trend Analysis

Exercise Concepts

A trend is an economic pattern that occurs over a fixed time. For example, a business owner may have noted the fluctuation in profits over several years. The owner will ask, "If this pattern continues, what profits or losses might result?" Excel can analyze such trends.

A trend is based on a pattern. A Linear pattern can be arithmetic (2, 4, 6, 8) or exponential (2, 4, 16, 256, 65536). You can specify a pattern by selecting worksheet cells that demonstrate the pattern. The =TREND function detects both of the these patterns and more complex patterns, like 1, -3, 8.25, 21.

You can also use the Series dialog box to create linear patterns. Select the cells that contain the pattern and the cells into which you want to continue the trend. When you select the Trend option in the dialog box, Excel analyzes the existing trend and extends it into the empty range.

Tips, Tricks, and Shortcuts

1. The syntax for the =TREND statistical function is: =TREND(*known_y's,known_x's, new_x's,const*). You must convert it to an array formula by pressing Shift + Control + Enter to ensure correct results.

2. The cell addresses that comprise the *known_y's* argument should remain relative references. The cell addresses that comprise the *known_x's* should be absolute. This allows you to save time by filling a working function into other cells.

3. You can also use the AutoFill feature to forecast a trend. Select the cells that contain the pattern and then click and drag the AutoFill handle to a new cell location to calculate the trend.

	City	1997	1998	1999	2000	2001	2002
6	Brea	19,556	21,155	20,199	20,946	21,268	21,589
7	Santa Ana	17,454	18,345	17,888			
8	Los Angeles	16,245	17,545	16,545			
9	Long Beach	26,657	27,896	27,796			

Figure 9.2: AutoFill used to calculate a trend

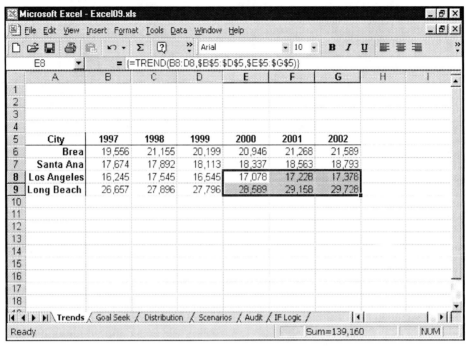

Figure 9.3: Analyzing trends

Exercise A: Employ Trend Analysis

5
4
3
2
1
Level of
Difficulty

Step by Step	Additional Information

1. Make sure Excel 2000 is open.

2. Select View to Toolbars to Customize....   The Customize dialog box opens.

3. Click the Options tab.

4. Select Reset my usage data under Personalized Menus and Toolbars.   To restore the default Toolbars.

5. Click Yes.

6. Click Close.   The Toolbars are restored.

7. Open Excel09.xls.   It is in the Temp folder on the desktop. When the workbook opens, The Trends worksheet is active.

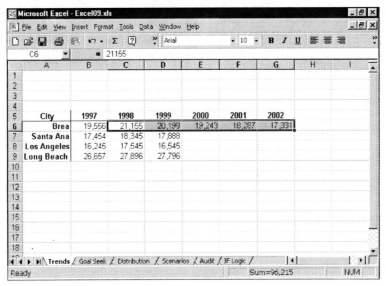

Figure 9.4: AutoFill used to calculate a decreasing trend

Step by Step	Additional Information

8. Select B6 to D6.

The trend for the franchise increased in 1998 but decreased in 1999.

9. Drag the AutoFill handle to G6.

A trend is extended. Sales continue to increase through the year 2002. See Figure 9.2.

10. Select C6 to D6.

You have selected a trend consisting of decreasing values. What if the sales continue to decrease after 1999?

11. Drag the AutoFill handle to G6.

The trend continues to decrease. See Figure 9.4.

12. Click the Undo button.

The increasing trend is restored. Notice that the series levels off in 2000, but continues through the year 2002.

13. Select B7 to G7.

14. Select Edit to Fill to Series....

The Series dialog box opens.

15. Make sure Linear is selected under Type.

You want to calculate a linear trend.

M9–8

Step by Step	Additional Information
16. Click Trend.	Make sure there is a check mark in the check box.
17. Click OK	A linear trend is calculated.
18. Click the Undo button.	The original series displays.
19. Select Edit to Fill to Series...	The Series dialog box opens.
20. Click Trend.	Make sure there is a check mark in the check box.
21. Select Growth under Type.	See Figure 9.5.
22. Click OK.	A growth trend series is calculated.
23. Select E8 to G8.	You will calculate a series using the =TREND function.
24. Type =TREND(.	
25. Select B8 to D8.	These cells contain the *known_y's*.
26. Press ,.	
27. Select B5 to D5.	These cells contain the *known_x's*.

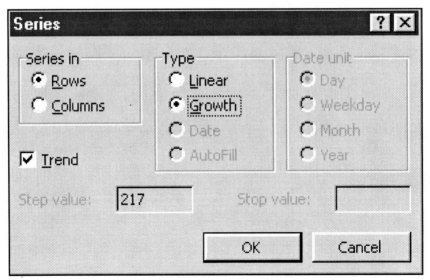

Figure 9.5: Calculating a growth trend

| DATE ▼ X ✓ = | =TREND(B8:D8,$B$5:$D$5,$E$5:$G$5 | | | | | | | | |

	A	B	C	D	E	F	G	H	I
1									
2									
3									
4									
5	City	1997	1998	1999	2000	2001	2002		
6	Brea	19,556	21,155	20,199	20,946	21,268	21,589		
7	Santa Ana	17,674	17,892	18,113	18,337	18,563	18,793		
8	Los Angeles	16,245	17,545	16,545	=TREND(B8:D8,$B$5:$D$5,$E$5:$G$5				
9	Long Beach	26,657	27,896	27,796					
10									
11									
12									
13									
14									

Figure 9.6: Defining arguments

Step by Step	Additional Information
28. Press F4.	Absolute referencing is applied to the cell addresses.
29. Press ,.	
30. Select E5 to G5.	You want to calculate a series of *new_x's* as a trend for these years.
31. Press F4.	Absolute referencing is applied to the cell addresses. See Figure 9.6.
32. Press Shift + Control + Enter.	The entry is converted to an array formula, and a series is calculated for the remaining cells in the row.
33. Drag the AutoFill handle to G9.	The relative references to the *known_y's* calculate a trend series for the remaining cells. See Figure 9.3.
34. Save your work.	
35. Leave this file open.	You will use it in the next exercise.

— User Notes—

Before You Begin Exercise B

Use Goal Seek

Exercise Concepts

A formula normally calculates a result based on numerical entries in a range. If the numerical entries are changed, the formula recalculates the result. However, what if you want the formula to calculate a specific total?

The result, which can be thought of as "working backwards," or backsolving, is known as a goal seek. Excel seeks the goal that you set when you force the total to change. The Goal Seek feature allows you to specify a formula-cell, a target value, and a variable cell for seeking a goal. Goal Seek solves the problem by adjusting the value in the adjustable cell until the formula calculates the specified result.

You must define three variables for a goal seek: the formula-cell, the value, and the adjustable cell. The formula-cell is the cell that contains the actual formula. The value is the result that you want the formula to calculate. The adjustable cell is the formula-dependent value that you want to change.

Tips, Tricks, and Shortcuts

1. Before opening the Goal Seek dialog box, select the cell that contains the formula which calculates the result; the *Set cell* field will contain the address of the formula cell.

2. Goal Seek overwrites the original value in the adjustable or changing cell. If you want to retain the original value, copy it to another location or save the file before using Goal Seek.

3. The Goal Seek option is found on the Tools menu.

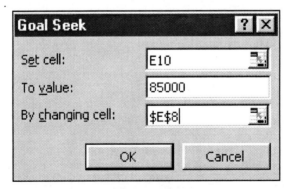

Figure 9.7: The Goal Seek dialog box

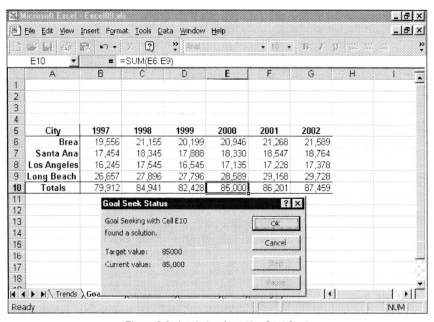

Figure 9.8: A solution found by Goal Seek

Exercise B: Use Goal Seek

5
4
3
2
1
Level of
Difficulty

Step by Step	Additional Information

Step by Step

1. Make sure Excel09.xls is open.

2. Click the Goal Seek sheet tab.

3. Click cell E10.

4. Select Tools to Goal Seek....

5. Drag the Goal Seek dialog box below row 10.

6. Click the To value: field.

7. Type 85000.

Additional Information

The Goal Seek worksheet becomes active.

This is the formula-cell. You want the formula in this cell to calculate the result *$85,000*.

The Goal Seek dialog box opens.

All of the data is visible.

This is the result, or value, that you want the formula to calculate.

Step by Step	Additional Information
8. Click the `By changing cell:` field.	
9. Click cell `E8`.	This is the adjustable or variable cell. You want to update the value in this cell until the formula-cell calculates the desired result. See Figure 9.7.
10. Click `OK`.	Goal Seek adjusts the value in cell E8 until the formula in E10 calculates the result *$85,000*. The Goal Seek Status dialog box opens. See Figure 9.8.
11. Click `OK`.	The desired total was calculated in cell E10.
12. Save your work.	
13. Leave this file open.	You will use it in the next exercise.

— User Notes—

Before You Begin Exercise C

Determine Frequency Distribution

Exercise Concepts

Frequency distribution, which is commonly used in market surveys and statistical analysis, ascertains the relationship between a range of values and a set of numeric intervals.

For example, perhaps you are conducting a market survey. When you conduct the poll, you ask each client to rate service on a scale of one to four. For every client polled, you want to know how many times each interval (rating) occurred. It is far more efficient to determine the distribution than to actually note the incidence of each value.

Determining the frequency distribution that occurs in a range requires some preparation. You must define two key areas – an input range and a bin range. The input range contains the numerical data that you want to evaluate. The bin range holds the numeric intervals through which the values are filtered, or distributed.

In this exercise, you will perform a frequency distribution analysis using the special Analysis ToolPak add-in.

Tips, Tricks, and Shortcuts

1. The intervals in the bin range must be in ascending order. Also, do not select labels or blank cells when defining the bin range.

2. If there are values in the Input Range that are outside the intervals defined in the Bin Range, they are reported in the More row of the frequency analysis.

3. Select the Histogram option from the Data Analysis dialog box to perform a frequency distribution analysis.

> To successfully complete this exercise, you must install the optional Analysis ToolPak add-in. See the preface for installation notes.

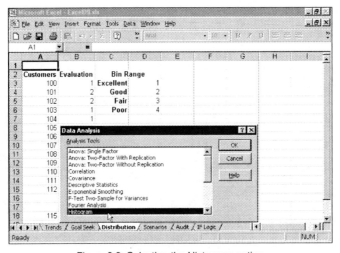

Figure 9.9: Selecting the Histogram option

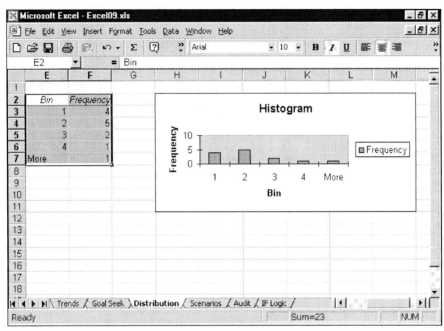

Figure 9.10: A frequency distribution analysis

Exercise C: Determine Frequency Distribution

| 5 |
| 4 |
| 3 |
| 2 |
| 1 |

Level of
Difficulty

Step by Step	**Additional Information**
1. Make sure Excel09.xls is open.	
2. Click the Distribution sheet tab.	The Distribution worksheet becomes active.
3. Select Tools to Add-Ins....	The Add-Ins dialog box opens.
4. Make sure Analysis ToolPak is selected.	Make sure there is a check mark in the check box.
5. Click OK.	
6. Select Tools to Data Analysis....	The Data Analysis dialog box opens.
7. Select Histogram.	See Figure 9.9.
8. Click OK.	The Histogram dialog box opens.

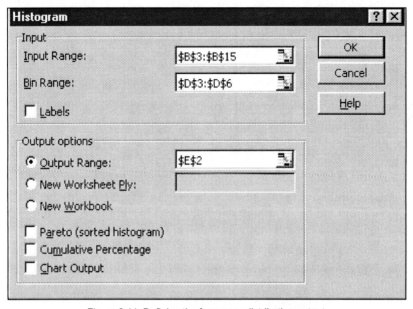

Figure 9.11: Defining the frequency distribution output

Step by Step	Additional Information
9. Click the Collapse Dialog button after Input Range: .	
10. Select B3 to B15 .	You want to determine the occurrence of each value in this range.
11. Press Enter .	The cell addresses appear in the Input Range field.
12. Click Collapse Dialog button after the Bin Range: field.	
13. Select D3 to D6 .	The Bin Range of intervals is defined.
14. Press Enter .	The cell addresses appear in the Bin Range field.
15. Select Output Range: under Output options .	
16. Click Collapse Dialog button after the Output Range: field.	
17. Click cell E2 .	

Step by Step	**Additional Information**
18. Press Enter.	The frequency distribution output will start in this cell. See Figure 9.11.
19. Click Chart Output under Output options.	Make sure there is a check mark in the check box.
20. Click OK.	Excel performs the frequency distribution analysis.
21. If necessary, scroll to view the output.	Each value's count, or frequency, displays in the Frequency column. The frequency was also charted. See Figure 9.10.
22. Save your work.	
23. Leave this file open.	You will use it in the next exercise.

Before You Begin Exercise D

Use Scenario Manager

Exercise Concepts

Each set of variables that you cycle through a "what-if" model is called a scenario. A scenario is a set of values that represents one possible outcome. For example, you might define one set of values as a "best-case" scenario and another as a "worst-case" scenario. The Scenario Manager allows you to save and name these versions for future reference.

You can save the values in each version in named ranges or absolute cell address references. You enter one set of data into the range and assign it a scenario name. You then save subsequent data sets with their own scenario names. The Scenario Manager allows you to cycle through the data sets and view the differences.

Tips, Tricks, and Shortcuts

1. You can use named ranges or absolute references in the *Changing cells* field area of the Scenario Manager.

2. The Scenario Values dialog box allows you to edit values for any defined scenario.

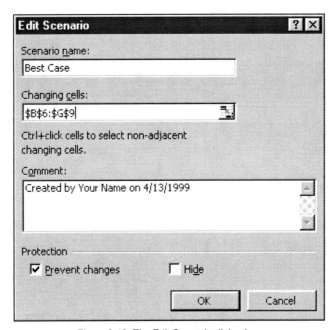

Figure 9.12: The Edit Scenario dialog box

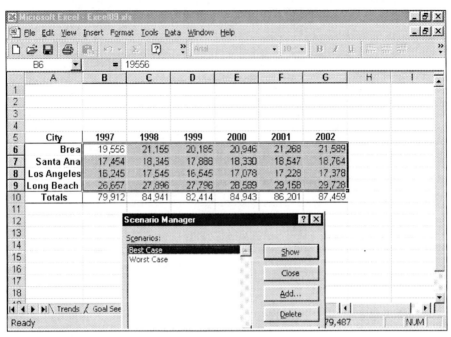

Figure 9.13: Managing scenarios

Exercise D: Use Scenario Manager

Level of
Difficulty

Step by Step	Additional Information
1. Make sure Excel09.xls is open.	
2. Click the Scenarios sheet tab.	The Scenarios worksheet becomes active.
3. Select Tools to Scenarios....	The Scenario Manager dialog box opens.
4. Click Add....	The Add Scenario dialog box opens.
5. Type Best Case.	To name the scenario.
6. Click the Collapse Dialog button.	
7. Select B6 to G9.	To define the changing cells.
8. Press Enter.	See Figure 9.12.
9. Click OK.	The Scenario Values dialog box opens.

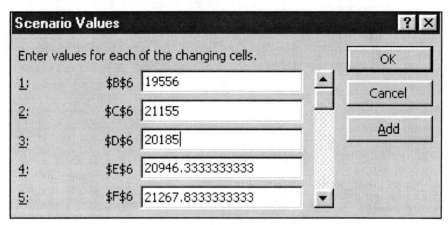

Figure 9.14: Editing changing values

Step by Step	Additional Information
10. Double-click the $D$6 field.	It is the third field listed.
11. Type 20185.	You can edit any scenarios' changing values. See Figure 9.14.
12. Click OK.	The Scenario Manager dialog box reappears.
13. Click Close.	
14. Select C6 to D9.	
15. Drag the AutoFill handle to G9.	A declining trend is calculated.
16. Select B6 to G9.	
17. Select Tools to Scenarios....	The Scenario Manager dialog box opens.
18. Click Add....	The Add Scenario dialog box opens.
19. Type Worst Case.	To name the declining trend scenario. See Figure 9.15.
20. Click OK twice.	The Scenario Manager dialog box reappears.
21. Select Best Case under Scenarios:.	
22. Click Show.	The Best Case scenario values display in the worksheet.

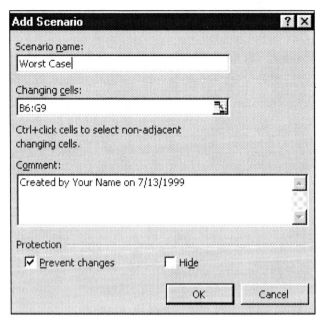

Figure 9.15: Naming and deleting the second scenario

Step by Step	Additional Information
23. If necessary, move the dialog box to display the results.	See Figure 9.13.
24. Click [Close].	
25. Save your work.	
26. Leave this file open.	You will use it in the next exercise.

Before You Begin Exercise E

Audit a Worksheet

Exercise Concepts

You can ensure the accuracy of formulas and find errors in complex worksheets with the Auditing options. When you audit a worksheet, Excel determines the relationships between formulas and the cells referenced by them.

Precedents are the cells that supply data to a formula, while dependents are cells that contain formulas which refer to other cells. When Excel locates either precedents or dependents, it applies tracer arrows to the cells. The tracer arrows display the relationship between the active cell and related cells.

When tracing precedents, you must select the formula cell before Excel can apply the tracer arrows. Likewise, a cell or range supplying data to a formula must be selected first when tracing dependents. If an error message, such as, #DIV/0! or #VALUE!, displays in a cell, you must select the cell before Excel can trace the error.

Tips, Tricks, and Shortcuts

1. You can use either the options on the Auditing submenu within the Tools menu or the Auditing toolbar to trace errors.

2. You must select a cell that contains a formula before you can trace precedents.

3. You must select a cell or range that supplies data to a formula before you can trace dependents.

4. You must select a cell that displays an error message before Excel can trace the error.

Figure 9.16: The Auditing toolbar

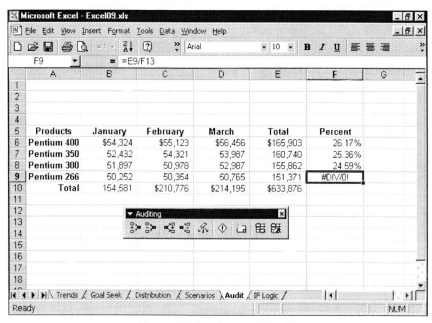

Figure 9.17: Opening an existing file

Exercise E: Audit a Worksheet

```
5
4
3
2
1
Level of
Difficulty
```

Step by Step	Additional Information
1. Make sure Excel09.xls is open.	
2. Click the Audit sheet tab.	The Audit worksheet becomes active.
3. Click cell B10.	You will trace the precedents.
4. Select Tools to Auditing to Trace Precedents.	A tracer arrow displays. Notice that cell B6 was omitted as a cell reference in the formula's arguments.
5. Select Tools to Auditing to Show Auditing Toolbar.	The Auditing toolbar displays. See Figure 9.16.
6. Drag the Auditing toolbar below row 10.	All of the data is visible.
7. Click cell B6.	

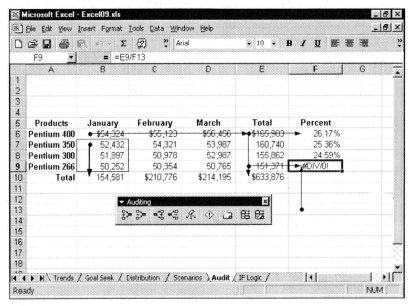

Figure 9.18: Tracing the errors in a worksheet

Step by Step	Additional Information

8. Click the Trace Dependents button.

 A tracer arrow displays finding the formula that refers to a specific cell.

9. Click cell E6.

10. Click the Trace Dependents button.

Tracer arrows display.

11. Click cell F9.

This cell displays an error message.

12. Click the Trace Error button.

Tracer arrows display. The formula refers to an empty cell, which causes the division error. See Figure 9.18.

13. Double-click cell F9.

The Formula displays in edit mode.

14. Select F13.

15. Type E10 Enter.

The Formula is fixed and the error is removed.

16. Click the Remove All Arrows button.

The tracer arrows are removed.

Step by Step	Additional Information
17. Select `File` to `Properties`.	You may need to click the arrow at the bottom of the menu to extend it. The Quarterly Sales.xls Properties dialog box opens.
18. Click the `Title:` field.	
19. Type `Quarterly Sales Report`.	To name the title for the properties.
20. Press `Tab` twice.	The Author: field is selected.
21. Type your name.	
22. Press `Tab` twice.	The Company: field is selected.
23. Type `The Computer Store`.	
24. Press `Tab` three times.	The Comments: field is selected.
25. Type `This is a report for the first Quarter.`.	To give the Properties sheet a comment about the workbook. See Figure 9.19.
26. Click `OK`.	You return to the worksheet.
27. Select `File` to `Exit`.	To close the file and exit Excel.

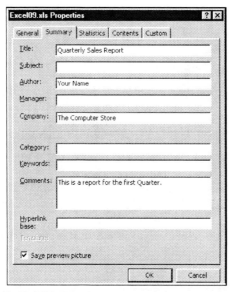

Figure 9.19: Changing the properties of a workbook

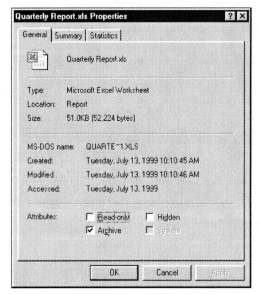

Figure 9.20: A long filename hashed to the DOS "8.3" file naming convention

Step by Step	Additional Information

28. Click `Yes`.

29. Double-click the `Temp` folder on the desktop.
The Temp window opens.

30. Right-click `Excel09.xls`.
A shortcut menu opens.

31. Select `Properties`.
The Quarterly Sales Report.xls Properties sheet opens. See Figure 9.20.

32. Note the `MS-DOS name:`.
It has been truncated, or hashed, to "QUARTE~1.XLS" for the purpose of backward compatibility.

33. Click the `Summary` tab.
The Quarterly Sales Report.xls Properties dialog box displays the contents of your workbook.

34. Click `OK`.
The property sheet closes.

35. Double-click `Excel09.xls`.
To start Excel and open the document. See Figure 9.17.

36. Leave this file open.
You will use this file in the next exercise.

— User Notes—

Before You Begin Exercise F

Use Data Validation

Exercise Concepts

Data validation provides a user with visual cues that indicate acceptable data types and values for a selected cell or range. If a user enters an invalid data type, an error message displays.

The Data Validation dialog box allows you to define the validation criteria, an input message, and an error message. The validation criteria can be any value, whole number, decimal, list, date, time, or text length. You can also define custom criteria parameters for valid data entries.

To audit a worksheet for invalid entries, click the Circle Invalid Data button on the Auditing toolbar. A red circle will appear around any entry that violates the validation criteria, and you can easily locate and correct the invalid entry.

Tips, Tricks, and Shortcuts

Click the Clear Validation Circles button on the Auditing toolbar to remove the circle and enter valid data in the cell.

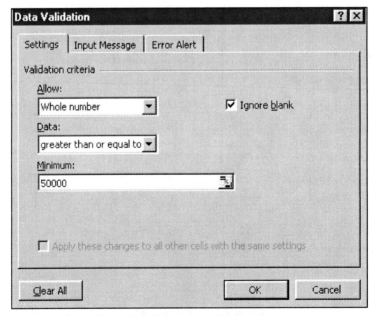

Figure 9.21: Defining the validation criteria

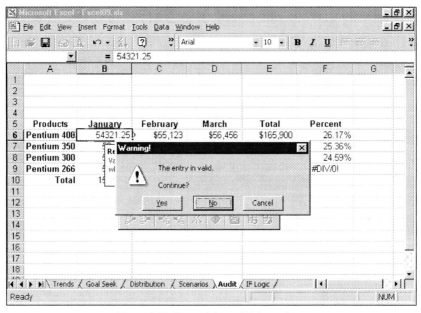

Figure 9.22: Determining valid data values

Exercise F: Use Data Validation

5
4
3
2
1

Level of
Difficulty

Step by Step	Additional Information
1. Make sure `Excel09.xls` is open.	
2. Make sure the `Audit` worksheet is active.	
3. Make sure the `Auditing` toolbar is active.	
4. Select `B6` to `D9`.	You will define data validation criteria for this range.
5. Select `Data` to `Validation...`.	The Data Validation dialog box opens.
6. Click the `Allow:` arrow.	A list of validation options opens.
7. Select `Whole number`.	The dialog box updates.

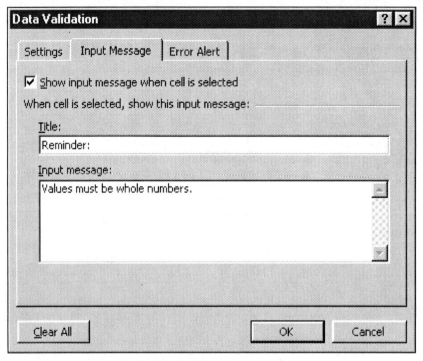

Figure 9.23: Defining the input message

Step by Step	Additional Information

8. Click the Data: arrow.

A list of conditional operators opens.

9. Select greater than or equal to.

10. Click the Minimum: field.

11. Type 50000.

The entry must be a whole number greater than or equal to this figure before it is accepted as a valid entry. See Figure 9.21.

12. Click the Input Message tab.

The dialog box updates.

13. Click the Title: field.

14. Type Reminder: Tab Values must be whole numbers..

See Figure 9.23.

Step by Step	Additional Information

15. Click the Error Alert tab.   The dialog box updates.

16. Click the Style: arrow.   A list of styles opens.

17. Select Warning.

18. Click the Title: field.

19. Type Warning! Tab The entry   See Figure 9.24.
    is invalid..

20. Click OK.   The dialog box closes. The input message that you
                       defined displays.

21. Click cell B6.

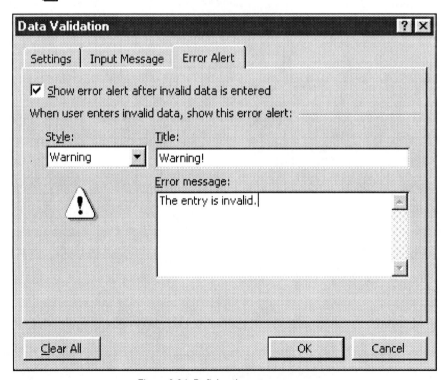

Figure 9.24: Defining the error message

Step by Step	Additional Information
22. Type `48987` `Enter`.	The warning message you defined displays.
23. Click `Yes`.	The entry is accepted.
24. Click the `Circle Invalid Data` button.	It is on the Auditing toolbar. The invalid entry is circled.
25. Click cell `B6`.	
26. Type `54321.25` `Enter`.	The warning message displays. While the value is greater than $50,000, it is not a whole number and is, therefore, invalid. See Figure 9.22.
27. Click `No`.	The cell's contents are selected.
28. Type `54321` `Enter`.	The entry matches the validation criteria. No warning message displays.
29. Save your work.	
30. Leave this file open.	You will use it in the next exercise.

— User Notes—

Before You Begin Exercise G

Nest an IF Function

Exercise Concepts

If you nest, or place one IF function within another, you can enhance the logical processing of the formula. Nested IF functions allow you to create refined logical tests.

For example, consider the following nested IF formula:

=IF(B24>10000,B24*B26,IF(B32>4,B24*B26,B24*F26))

This test depends on whether or not the value in B24 is greater than 10,000. If it is, the formula multiplies B24 by another value in B26. However, if the value is 10,000 or less, the nested IF tests the value in B32. If B32 is greater than 4, B24 is multiplied by B26. If the value in B32 is 4 or less, B24 is multiplied by F26.

You can nest up to seven IF functions within one formula. The use of nested IFs relies on your ability to keep track of how to use the value arguments and correct syntax.

Tips, Tricks, and Shortcuts

In nested IF formulas, one expressed statement is contained within another, using the following syntax:

=IF(*logical_test,value_if_true*,IF(*logical_test,value_if_true,value_if_false*)).

	A	B	C	D	E
1					
2	Gross Sales:	$ 9,500.00			
3					
4	High Bonus:	7.00%		Low Bonus:	3.00%
5					
6	Bonus:	$ 285.00			
7					
8	Number of Months:				

Figure 9.25: Results of an IF functions formula

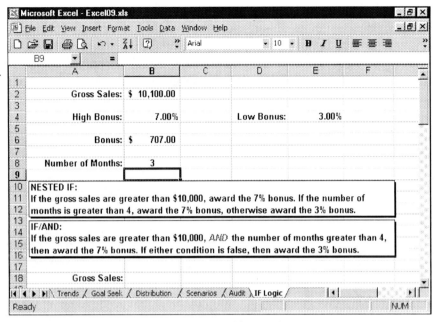

Figure 9.26: A nested IF function formula

Exercise G: Nest an IF Function

Level of
Difficulty

Step by Step	Additional Information

1. Make sure Excel09.xls is open.

2. Click the IF Logic sheet tab.   The IF Logic worksheet becomes active.

3. Close the Auditing toolbar.

4. Click cell B2.

5. Type 9500 Enter.

6. Click cell B6.

7. Type
=IF(B2>10000,B2*B4,IF(B8>4,
B2*B4,B2*E4)).

   If the sales amount is greater than $10,000, award the higher bonus. If the number of months is greater than 4, award the high bonus no matter what the sales amount.

Step by Step	Additional Information
8. Press Enter.	The result, $285.00, displays in B6. What if you enter the number of months? See Figure 9.25.
9. Click cell B8.	
10. Type 4 Enter.	The result remains unchanged. The number of months must be greater than four.
11. Click cell B8.	
12. Type 5 Enter.	The result, $665.00, displays. Even though the sales were below $10,000, the nested IF calculates the higher bonus.
13. Click cell B2.	
14. Type 10100 Enter.	The bonus increases to $707.00. What happens if the number of months is less than four?
15. Click cell B8.	
16. Type 3 Enter.	The result remains unchanged. While the number of months is less than four, the amount of sales is greater than $10,000, so the high bonus is awarded. See Figure 9.26.
17. Save your work.	
18. Leave this file open.	You will use it in the next exercise.

— User Notes—

Before You Begin Exercise H

Combine Logical Functions

Exercise Concepts

While nested IF functions can perform refined tests, you can create more efficient formulas by combining other logical functions with the IF function. These other logical functions are AND, OR, and NOT.

The correct syntax for combining any logical function with the IF function is as follows:

=IF(*logical_function_name*(*logical_test*,*value_if_true*,*value_if_false*).

The AND logical function requires that all conditions being tested return a value of "true." If all the conditions are true, then the IF formula displays the *value_if_true* statement. If any of the conditions fail the test, then the *value_if_false* statement is calculated.

The OR logical function tests the multiple conditions to determine if any of them are true. If either condition tests true, then the *value_if_true* statement is calculated. If neither condition tests true, then the *value_if_false* statement displays.

A NOT logical function formula returns a reverse value for the conditions tested. In this sense, a true condition is displayed as false, and vice versa. You can use NOT when you want to ensure that a value is not equal to one particular value.

Tips, Tricks, and Shortcuts

The three logical function formulas you will write for the exercise appear in this order:

- =IF(AND(B2>10000,B8>4),B2*B4,B2*E4)
  The AND function in this formula ensures that both statements must be true. The value in B2 must be greater than 10,000 and the value in B8 greater than 4 before B2 is multiplied by B4. If either statement is false, B2 is multiplied by E4.

- =IF(OR(B18>10000,B24>4)B18*B20,B18*E20)
  The OR function tests both values in B18 and B24, either of which can be true to multiply B18 by B20. If neither are true, then B18 is multiplied by E20.

- =IF(NOT(B18>10000),B18*B20,B18*E20)
  The NOT function returns the reverse value for the condition in B18. While B18 may be greater than 10,000, NOT multiplies B18 by E20 rather than B18 by B20.

DATE	▼ X √ =	=IF(AND(B2>10000,B8>4),B2*B4,B2*E4)			
	A	B	C	D	E
1					
2	Gross Sales:	$ 10,100.00			
3					
4	High Bonus:	7.00%		Low Bonus:	3.00%
5					
6	Bonus:	=IF(AND(B2>10000,B8>4),B2*B4,B2*E4)			
7					
8	Number of Months:	3			

Figure 9.27: The AND logic function

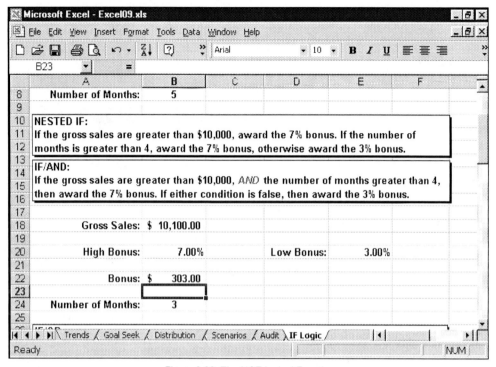

Figure 9.28: The NOT logical Function

Exercise H: Combine Logical Functions

Level of
Difficulty

Step by Step	Additional Information
1. Make sure `Excel09.xls` is open.	
2. Make sure the `IF Logic` worksheet is active.	
3. Click cell `B6`.	
4. Press `Delete`.	You will write a more efficient formula using the AND logical function.
5. Type `=IF(AND(B2>10000,B8>4) ,B2*B4,B2*E4)`.	The AND logical function is testing two conditions, both of which must be true. The gross sales must be greater than $10,000 and the number of months greater than four. See Figure 9.27.

DATE	▼	✗ ✓ =	=IF(OR(B18>10000,B24>4),B18*B20,B18*E20)		
	A	B	C	D	E
17					
18	Gross Sales:	$ 10,100.00			
19					
20	High Bonus:	7.00%		Low Bonus:	3.00%
21					
22	Bonus:	=IF(OR(B18>10000,B24>4),B18*B20,B18*E20)			
23					
24	Number of Months:				

Figure 9.29: The OR logical function

Step by Step	Additional Information
6. Press [Enter].	The result, $303.00, displays in B4. The sales are greater than $10,000, but the number of months is less than four.
7. Click cell [B8].	
8. Type 5 [Enter].	The result, $707.00, displays. Now that both conditions are true, the higher rate is calculated.
9. Scroll to and click cell [B18].	
10. Type 10100 [Enter].	
11. Click cell [B22].	
12. Type =IF(OR(B18>10000,B24>4),B18*B20,B18*E20).	The OR logical function is testing two conditions, either of which can be true. If either the gross sales are greater than $10,000 or the number of months greater than four, the higher bonus is calculated. See Figure 9.29.
13. Press [Enter].	The result, $707.00, displays. While there is no value for the number of months, the sales are greater than $10,000.
14. Click cell [B24].	
15. Type 5 [Enter].	The result remains unchanged.
16. Click cell [B18].	

Step by Step	Additional Information

17. Type 9500 [Enter].
    The result still reflects a calculation by the high bonus rate.

18. Click cell [B24].

19. Type 3 [Enter].
    The result now reflects a calculation by the low bonus rate. Neither condition was found to be true.

20. Click cell [B18].

21. Type 10100 [Enter].

22. Click cell [B22].

23. Type
    =IF(NOT(B18>10000),B18*B20,
    B18*E20).
    The NOT logical function returns the reverse value for the condition tested. See Figure 9.30.

24. Press [Enter].
    Though the sales are greater than $10,000, NOT calculates the sales by the lower bonus rate. See Figure 9.28.

25. Save your work.

26. Close the file.

27. Select [File] to [Exit].
    You have completed this module.

DATE	▼ X ✓ =	=IF(NOT(B18>10000),B18*B20,B18*E20)		
	A	B	C	D	E
17					
18	Gross Sales:	$ 10,100.00			
19					
20	High Bonus:	7.00%		Low Bonus:	3.00%
21					
22	Bonus:	=IF(NOT(B18>10000),B18*B20,B18*E20)			
23					
24	Number of Months:	3			

Figure 9.30: The NOT logical function

Before You Begin Exercise I

Use Conditional Formatting

Exercise Concepts

Conditional formatting serves as a visual guide and allows a user to monitor changes in dynamic values. If data matches certain conditions, or criteria, then Excel applies a user-defined format to the cell contents. A conditional format can be applied to a cell or to a range.

The Conditional Formatting dialog box allows you to specify up to three conditions. The *Cell Value Is* option formats cell contents based on their values, while the *Formula Is* option evaluates formulas that return true or false statements. The default selection is the former option.

You must specify a comparison operator to define the condition on the selected range. You can specify eight operators: *between, not between, equal to, not equal to, greater than, less than, greater than or equal to, and less than or equal to.*

Once you have specified the criteria, you must define the formatting to be applied to the contents of cells that match the criteria. Font styles, colors, borders, and patterns can be applied as conditional formats.

Tips, Tricks, and Shortcuts

1. Select the Conditional Formatting option from the Format menu to open the Conditional Formatting dialog box.

2. Click the Format button in the Conditional Formatting dialog box to access the Format Cells dialog box.

3. You can specify up to three conditions for a selected range or cell.

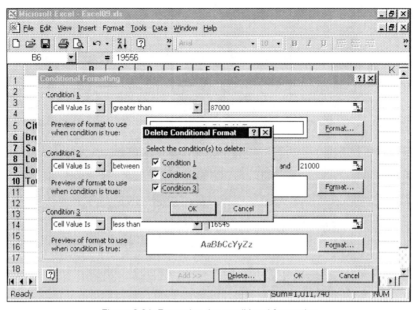

Figure 9.31: Removing the conditional formatting

Exercise I: Use Conditional Formatting

Level of Difficulty
5
4
3
2
1

Step by Step	Additional Information
1. Make sure Excel09.xls is open.	
2. Select the Scenarios sheet tab.	You will apply conditional formatting to this range.
3. Select cells A5 to G10.	
4. Select Format to AutoFormat... .	The AutoFormat dialog box opens.
5. Select 3D Effects1.	
6. Press Enter.	
7. Select cells B6 to G10.	
8. Select Format to Conditional Formatting... .	The Conditional Formatting dialog box opens.
9. If necessary, click No, don't provide help now on the Office Assistant.	

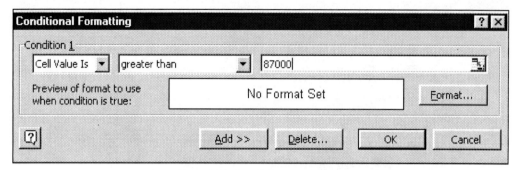

Figure 9.32: Specifying the condition

Step by Step	Additional Information
10. Make sure Cell Value Is is selected under Condition 1.	You want to evaluate cell values, not logical formulas.
11. Click the comparison operator arrow.	⬜ between ▼ A list of comparison operators opens.
12. Select greater than.	The dialog box updates.
13. Press Tab.	
14. Type 87000.	You want to apply conditional formatting to all values greater than 87,000. See Figure 9.32.
15. Click Format....	The Format Cells dialog box opens.
16. If necessary, click the Font tab.	
17. Select Bold under Font style:.	
18. Click the Color: arrow.	A color palette opens.
19. Select the Red color.	
20. Click the Border tab.	The dialog box updates.
21. Click the Outline button.	The sample area updates.
22. Click the Patterns tab.	The dialog box updates.
23. Click the white square under Color:.	To apply a white background to the cell. See Figure 9.33.
24. Click OK.	You return to the Conditional Formatting dialog box. The preview area displays the selected formatting.

Step by Step	Additional Information

25. Click OK.

26. Click cell G10.

To view the changes. The formatting updated for the cell containing a value that matched the criteria.

27. Select B6 to G10.

28. Select Format to Conditional Formatting....

The Conditional Formatting dialog box opens.

29. Click Add>>.

The dialog box updates. You will specify a second condition.

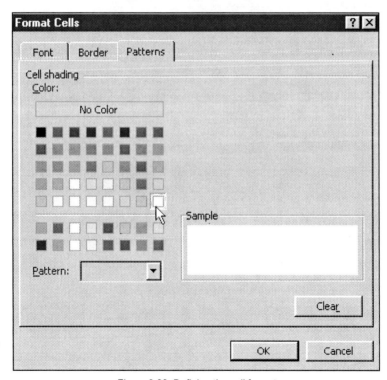

Figure 9.33: Defining the cell format

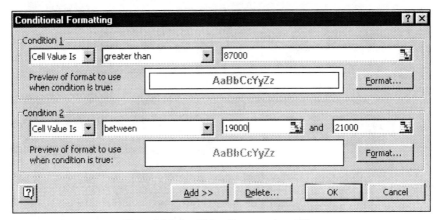

Figure 9.34: Specifying the second condition

Step by Step	**Additional Information**

30. Make sure between is the Condition 2 conditional operator.

31. Type Tab Tab 19000 Tab 21000.

You want to apply conditional formatting to data between these values. See Figure 9.34.

32. Click Format... under Condition 2.

The Format Cells dialog box opens. The Patterns section is still active.

33. Click the white square under Color:.

34. Click the Font tab.

The dialog box updates.

35. Select Bold under Font style:.

36. Select Blue under Color:.

37. Click OK twice.

To close both dialog boxes.

38. Click cell A1.

To view the changes. Conditional formatting was applied to the values matching the criteria.

39. Select B6 to G10.

40. Select Format to Conditional Formatting....

The Conditional Formatting dialog box opens.

41. Click Add>>.

The dialog box updates. You will specify a third condition.

Step by Step	Additional Information

42. Click the `Condition 3` comparison operator arrow.

between ▼   A list of comparison operators opens.

43. Select `less than`.

44. Type `Tab` 16545.

You want to apply conditional formatting to data below this value.

45. Click `Format...` under `Condition 3`.

The Format Cells dialog box opens. The Font section is active.

46. Select `Bold Italic` under `Font style:`.

47. Select `Red` under `Color:`.

48. Click `OK`.

You return to the Conditional Formatting dialog box. The preview area displays the selected format. See Figure 9.35.

49. Click `OK`.

50. Click cell `B8`.

This value matches the third conditional formatting criterion.

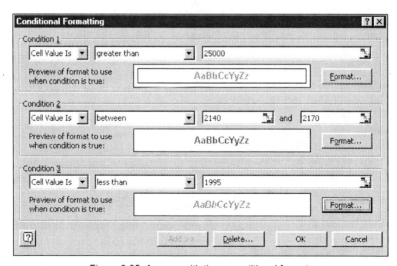

Figure 9.35: A range with three conditional formats

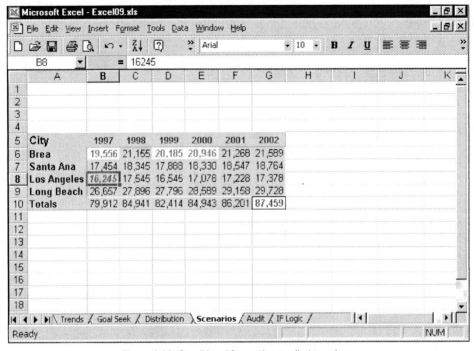

Figure 9.36: Conditional formatting applied to values

Step by Step	Additional Information
51. Type 16600 [Enter].	The conditional formatting is removed. The value no longer matches the criterion.
52. Click the [Undo] button.	The last action is undone. The conditional formatting is applied. See Figure 9.36.
53. Select [B6] to [G10].	
54. Select [Format] to [Conditional Formatting...].	The Conditional Formatting dialog box opens.
55. Click [Delete...].	The Delete Conditional Format dialog box opens.
56. Select [Condition 1], [Condition 2], and [Condition 3].	Make sure there are check marks in the check boxes. You will remove the conditional formatting. See Figure 9.31.
57. Click [OK].	The dialog box updates.

M9–50

Step by Step	Additional Information
58. Click OK.	
59. Click cell A1.	The conditional formatting was removed.
60. Save your work.	
61. Select File to Exit.	You have completed this module.

Module Review

True or False

1. An IF function formula has three arguments: the test, an "if true" statement, and an "if false" statement.

2. IF functions can be nested within one another.

3. The AND logical function tests multiple conditions, of which any can be true.

4. IF functions cannot display text strings; they can only calculate results.

5. The NOT logical function returns the reverse value for the condition tested.

Multiple Choice

6. Goal Seek finds a solution by...
   a. changing the formula cell.
   b. adjusting the value in a single cell.
   c. adjusting the values in multiple cells.
   d. none of the above

7. The correct syntax for the AND function in an IF logical formula is
   a. =AND(IF(B2>10000,B8>4),B2*B4,B2*E4)
   b. =AND(=IF(B2>10000,B8>4),B2*B4,B2*E4)
   c. =IF(AND(B2>10000,B8>4),B2*B4,B2*E4)
   d. =(IF/AND((B2>10000,B8>4),B2*B4,B2*E4))

1. True; 2. True; 3. False; 4. False; 5. True; 6. b.; 7. c.

Study Guide

This study guide presents the skills mastered in this module. As a means of review, assess your comprehension for each skill.

Are you proficient in these skills?

Topic	Yes	Need Review
Employ Trend Analysis	❑	❑
Use Goal Seek	❑	❑
Determine Frequency Distribution	❑	❑
Use Scenario Manager	❑	❑
Audit a Worksheet	❑	❑
Use Data Validation	❑	❑
Nest an IF Function	❑	❑
Combine Logical Functions	❑	❑
Use Conditional Formatting	❑	❑

To test your understanding of the concepts presented in this module, try the following:

Determine the profits or losses of your business for the past three years. Enter the values into a worksheet. Predict the trend for the next three years, calculating linear and growth patterns. Use the Scenario Manager to track and display the different outcomes.

— User Notes —

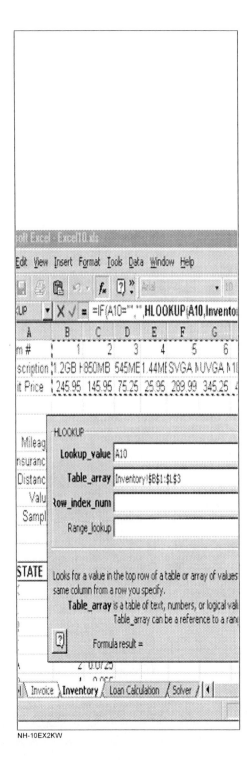

Advanced
Excel 2000 for Windows 95

MODULE

10

Advanced Data Management

Excel's data tables and lookup functions allow you to retrieve information with ease. You can create complex one- and two-variable data tables for data analysis.

— User Notes —

Module Preview: What-IF Tables

While a worksheet program is very useful for organizing numerical data, locating information, especially in large worksheets, can sometimes be difficult. To solve this problem, Excel can find data based on search criteria.

If data is in a table, you can extract it using lookup functions. Functions, such as HLOOKUP and VLOOKUP, can help you track many different kinds of data. You can use lookup functions to search for sales figures, addresses, telephone numbers, and just about anything else. If you have a database with hundreds of records, you will definitely need to utilize lookup functions.

If you need to analyze data that is influenced by variables, Excel can assist you as well. For example, you may want to analyze the cost of a loan with varying interest rates, amounts, and terms. You may want to determine the effect of discounts on inventory and sales, or you may want to calculate the commission for an account executive. For this type of analysis, you can create "what-if" tables with one or two variables. You can use these tables to instantly calculate the effects that different variables have on your figures.

You can also employ "what-if" tables to calculate scenarios. "What if" tables allow you to answer complex questions like, "What if I need to borrow "X" amount of dollars?" or "What if I discount all my inventory by twenty percent?".

You can also employ Solver to find the best solution to your problem. For example, what if you need to determine how much to sell in the fourth quarter to reach your year end goal? Since some products do not sell as well as other products, what do you do? Solver will put constraints on the products that do not sell well and adjust the other products that do sell well to meet your year end goal.

	A	B	C	D	E	F	G	H
					D8	=	=D7*12	
1								
2			Amount of Loan	$ (325,000.00)		If Interest Is	Monthly Payment	
3			APR	7.50%			Will Be	
4			Monthly Interest Rate	0.63%			$ 2,618.18	
5						4.0%	$ 1,969.44	
6						4.3%	$ 2,012.51	
7			Number of Years	20		4.5%	$ 2,056.11	
8			Conversion to Months	240		4.8%	$ 2,100.23	
9						5.0%	$ 2,144.86	
10			Monthly Payment	$2,618.18		5.3%	$ 2,189.99	
11						5.5%	$ 2,235.63	
12			Total Dollars Paid	$ 628,362.69		5.8%	$ 2,281.77	
13						6.0%	$ 2,328.40	
14						6.3%	$ 2,375.52	
15						6.5%	$ 2,423.11	
16						6.8%	$ 2,471.18	
17						7.0%	$ 2,519.72	
18						7.3%	$ 2,568.72	

Invoice / Inventory \ Loan Calculation / Solver /

Figure .1: An Excel data table

— User Notes —

Module Objectives

Upon completion of this module,
you will master the skills necessary to:

A.   Use HLOOKUP

B.   Use VLOOKUP

C.   Create a One-Variable Data Table

D.   Create a Two-Variable Data Table

E.   Use Solver

Before You Begin Exercise A

Use HLOOKUP

Exercise Concepts

If you use a worksheet as a data table for reporting changing information, you will find lookup functions very useful. A horizontal lookup function operates by searching the top row of a data table from left to right. Once the horizontal lookup function finds a label that matches the lookup value in a comparison cell, the horizontal lookup function moves down the column.

The syntax of the HLOOKUP function is: HLOOKUP (*lookup_value,table_array,row_index_num,range_ lookup*).

The HLOOKUP function has four sets of arguments:

1. The *lookup_value* argument is the reference or address of the comparison cell.

2. The *table_array* argument is the data-table range that is searched.

3. The *row_index_num* argument indicates how many cells to move down (must be 1 or greater).

4. The *range_lookup* argument is a logical argument that returns a true or false value. This argument is optional.

Tips, Tricks, and Shortcuts

1. f_{x} You can use the Paste Function feature to easily define the arguments and to paste the function into a specific cell or nest it into a logical IF function formula.

2. You can also combine the HLOOKUP function with the logical function IF to create a conditional test of the *lookup_value* cell's contents.

	Item Number	Description	Unit Price	Quantity	Extended Price	
9						
10	MAD00Y01				$ 0.00	
11	MAD00Y02				$ 0.00	
12						
13						

Figure 10.2: Adding values to a custom format

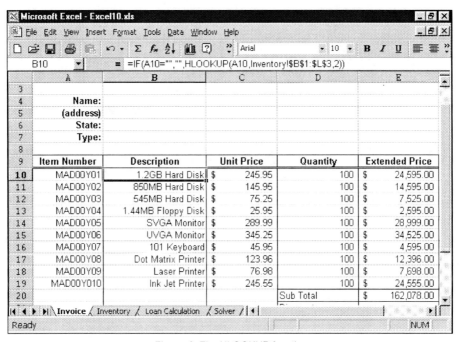

Figure .3: The HLOOKUP function

Exercise A: Use HLOOKUP

5
4
3
2
1

Level of
Difficulty

Step by Step	Additional Information
1. Make sure Excel 2000 is open.	
2. Close all open files.	
3. Select View to Toolbars to Customize....	The Customize dialog box opens.
4. Click the Options tab.	
5. Select Reset my usage data under Personalized Menus and Toolbars.	To restore the default Toolbars.
6. Click Yes.	
7. Click Close.	The Toolbars are restored.

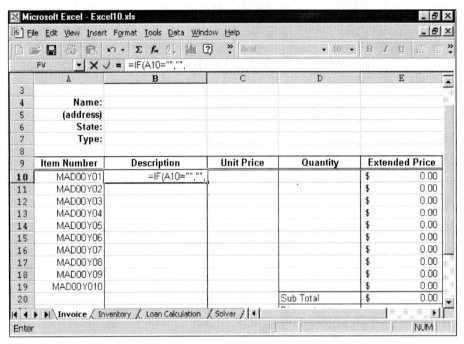

Figure 10.4: Testing the condition of a cell

Step by Step	Additional Information
8. Open Excel10.xls.	Excel10.xls is located in the Temp folder on the desktop. When the document opens, the Invoice worksheet is active.
9. Click cell A10.	
10. Type **1** Enter **2** Enter.	A custom format in the cells adds a series of characters to the values. See Figure 10.2.
11. Select A10 to A11.	
12. Drag the AutoFill handle to A19.	Click and drag the AutoFill handle of the cell selector to A19. A series, 1 to 10, is created.
13. Click cell E10.	The IF function formulas contained in this column test whether or not the cell in column A contains entries.
14. Click cell B10.	

Step by Step	Additional Information

15. Type =IF(A10="","",.

Do not type the period. This part of the formula tests whether or not column A contains entries. See Figure 10.4.

16. Click the `Paste Function` button.

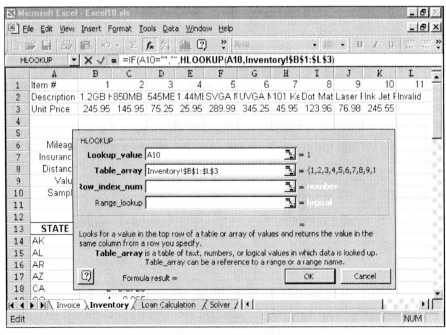 The Paste Function button is in the Standard toolbar. The Paste Function dialog box opens.

17. If the `Office Assistant` appears, click `No`.

The Office Assistant closes.

18. Select `Lookup & Reference` under `Function category:`.

You will insert the HLOOKUP function into the formula.

19. Select `HLOOKUP` under `Function name:`.

20. Click `OK`.

The Formula Palette opens.

Figure 10.5: Defining HLOOKUP arguments

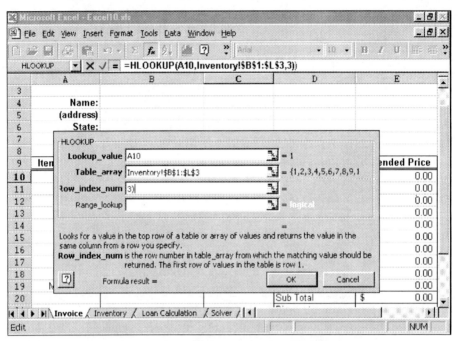

Figure 10.6: HLOOKUP nested within IF formula

Step by Step	Additional Information

21. Type **A10** `Tab`.

This is the lookup value argument.

22. Click the `Inventory` sheet tab.

The Inventory worksheet becomes active.

23. Drag the `Formula Palette` down until you can view the `Description` and `Unit Price` rows.

24. Select `B1` to `L3`.

This is the table array argument.

25. Press `F4`.

Absolute referencing is applied to the cell addresses. See Figure 10.5.

26. Type `Tab` **2)**.

This is the row index number argument. You want HLOOKUP to search the second row that contains the description for each item.

27. Click `OK`.

The formula is completed. The result, 1.2GB Hard Disk, displays.

M10–10

Step by Step	Additional Information

28. Drag the AutoFill handle to B19. | The HLOOKUP in the formula matches the values in column A, the item numbers, with the item names in the table.

29. Click cell C10. | You will use HLOOKUP to find the unit price for each item.

30. Type =IF(A10="","",. |

31. Click the Paste Function button. | The Paste Function dialog box opens.

32. Select HLOOKUP under Function name:. |

33. Click OK. | The Formula Palette opens.

34. Type A10 Tab. | This is the lookup value argument.

35. Click the Inventory sheet tab. | The Inventory worksheet becomes active.

36. Drag the Formula Palette down until you can view the Description and Unit Price rows. |

37. Select B1 to L3. |

38. Press F4. | Absolute referencing is applied to the cell addresses.

39. Type Tab 3). | You want HLOOKUP to search the row, number 3, that contains the unit price for each item. See Figure 10.6.

40. Click OK. | The formula returns the value for the unit price of "1.2GB Hard Disk."

41. Drag the AutoFill handle to C19. | The HLOOKUP function returns the unit price for all the items.

42. Click cell D10. |

43. Type 100 Enter, Up Arrow. |

44. Drag the AutoFill handle to D19. | The formulas in the Extended Price column calculate results. What if there is no entry in cell A10?

Step by Step	Additional Information
45. Click cell `A10`.	
46. Press `Delete`.	Since there is no entry in A10, the formula cells in the row become blank.
47. Type 1 `Tab`.	The formula cells calculate results. See Figure 10.3.
48. Save your work.	
49. Leave this file open.	You will use it in the next exercise.

— User Notes—

Before You Begin Exercise B

Use VLOOKUP

Exercise Concepts

A vertical lookup works in a similar fashion to a horizontal lookup. The VLOOKUP searches the data table vertically (from top to bottom), trying to match the comparison information.

VLOOKUP uses four sets of arguments, the last of which is optional. The syntax of the function is:

VLOOKUP(*lookup_value,table_array,col_index_num,range_lookup*).

1. The *lookup_value* argument is the reference or address of the comparison cell.

2. The *table_array* argument is the data-table range to be searched.

3. The *col_index_num* argument indicates how many columns right to move after a matching label is located.

4. The optional argument, *range_lookup*, is a logical value, either true or false, that specifies an exact match. If the argument is omitted, VLOOKUP returns the closest approximate match in the table.

Tips, Tricks, and Shortcuts

1. ![fx] You can use the Paste Function feature to easily define the arguments and paste the function into a specific cell or to nest it into a logical IF function formula.

2. You can also combine the VLOOKUP function with the logical function IF to create a conditional test of the *lookup_value* cell's contents.

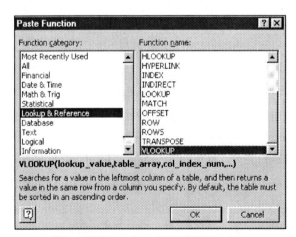

Figure 10.7: Inserting a VLOOKUP function

© New Horizons Publishing Center

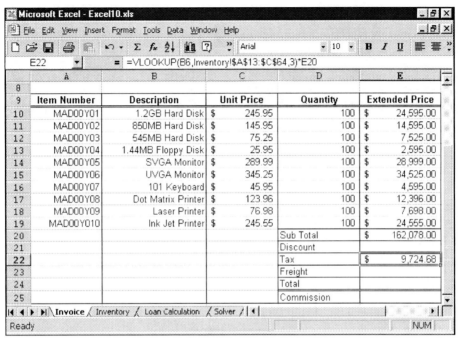

Figure .8: The VLOOKUP function

Exercise B: Use VLOOKUP

5
4
3
2
1

Level of
Difficulty

Step by Step	Additional Information

1. Make sure `Excel10.xls` is open.

2. Make sure the `Invoice` worksheet is active.

3. Click cell `B6`.

4. Type **CA** `Enter`. — You will create a VLOOKUP formula that locates a state's specific tax and multiplies it by the subtotal.

5. Scroll to and click cell `E22`.

6. Click the `Paste Function` button. — The Paste Function dialog box opens.

7. Select `Lookup & Reference` under `Function Catagory:`.

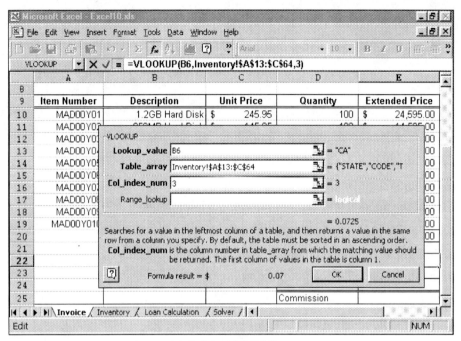

Figure 10.9: Defining VLOOKUP arguments

Step by Step	Additional Information
8. Press `Tab`.	
9. Press `V`.	The VLOOKUP function is selected. See Figure 10.7.
10. Click `OK`.	The Formula Palette opens.
11. Type **B6** `Tab`.	This is the lookup value argument.
12. Click the `Inventory` sheet tab.	The Inventory worksheet becomes active.
13. Drag the `Formula Palette` to the right until you can view the `A` column.	
14. Select `A14` to `C64`.	
15. Press `F4`.	Absolute referencing is applied to the table array argument.
16. Type `Tab` **3**.	See Figure 10.9.

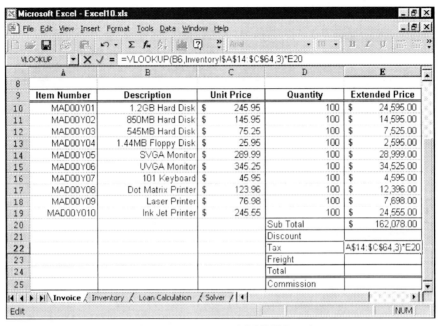

Figure 10.10: An edited VLOOKUP formula

Step by Step	Additional Information
17. Click OK.	
18. Click after the formula in the Formula bar.	
19. Type *E20.	You want to multiply the returned tax by the subtotal to calculate the full amount. See Figure 10.10.
20. Press Enter.	
21. Scroll to and click cell B6.	
22. Type AZ Enter.	
23. Scroll to and click cell E22.	The VLOOKUP function returns the tax for sales to customers in Arizona. See Figure 10.8.
24. Save your work.	
25. Leave this file open.	You will use it in the next exercise.

Before You Begin Exercise C

Create a One-Variable Data Table

Exercise Concepts

In analyzing many types of "what-if" questions, you need to use a Data table. For example, a data table can answer the questions, "What if I borrow $245,000 at 6% interest and repay it over 30 years? What's the monthly payment?".

Only one variable (such as, the term, amount borrowed, or interest rate) changes in a one-variable data table. You can alter this single variable in a cell connected to the table and view the results of various rates, repayment terms, or loan amounts. If you create the area that contains the desired financial (or other) information near the one-variable data table, it is easier to change the variable and view the results. The cell that you change in this area is called the input cell. You can then enter a sample figure as a place holder in the top row of the table. This is the only item the table's top row can contain.

Tips, Tricks, and Shortcuts

1. Do not change the cell in the comparison area that is designated as the row or column input cell. This changes the top-row example but not the table itself.

2. You can use either the AutoFill feature or the Series command to create the table's left column.

	A	B	C	D	E
1					
2			Amount of Loan	$ (325,000.00)	
3			APR	7.50%	
4		Monthly Interest Rate		0.63%	
5					
6					
7			Number of Years	30	
8		Conversion to Months		360	
9					
10		Monthly Payment			
11					
12		Total Dollars Paid			
13					

Figure 10.11: Converting the years to months

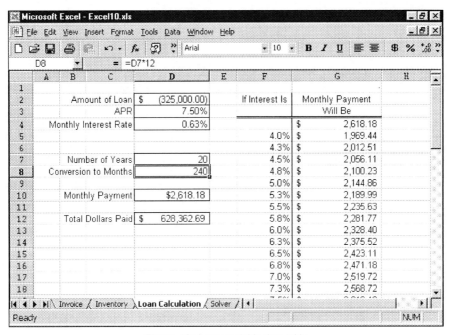

Figure .12: A one-variable data table

Exercise C: Create a One-Variable Data Table

Level of
Difficulty

Step by Step	Additional Information

1. Make sure Excel10.xls is open.

2. Click the Loan Calculation sheet tab.   The Loan Calculation worksheet becomes active.

3. Click cell D2.

4. Type -325000 Enter.   The amount being borrowed is entered as a negative number.

5. Click cell D7.

6. Type 30 Enter.   The length of the term.

7. Type =D7*12 Enter.   This formula converts the years to months. See Figure 10.11.

8. Click cell D10.

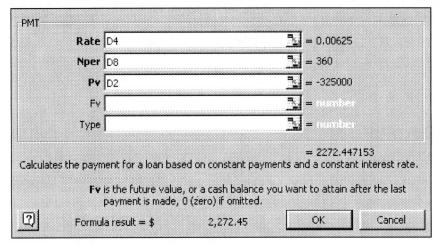

Figure 10.13: Calculating a monthly payment

Step by Step	Additional Information
9. Click the `Paste Function` button.	The Paste Function dialog box opens.
10. Select `Financial` under `Function category:`.	
11. Select `PMT` under `Function name:`.	This function calculates a monthly payment.
12. Click `OK`.	The Formula Palette opens.
13. Type **D4** `Tab` **D8** `Tab` **D2** `Tab`.	The function's arguments are defined. See Figure 10.13.
14. Click `OK`.	The formula calculates a result.
15. Click cell `D12`.	
16. Type **=D8*D10** `Enter`.	The formula calculates the total amount paid over the term.
17. Click cell `F5`.	
18. Type **0.04** `Enter`, then `Up Arrow`.	You will create a series of percentages.
19. Select `Edit` to `Fill` to `Series...`.	The Series dialog box opens.
20. Select `Columns` under `Series in`.	You want to create the series down the column.
21. Double-click the `Step value:` field.	

Step by Step	Additional Information
22. Type .0025 Tab .12.	See Figure 10.14.
23. Press Enter.	A series of percentage rates are calculated; this is the left column of the table.
24. Click cell G4.	
25. Type =PMT(D4,D8,D2) Enter.	A result displays in cell G4. The formula will be used as one variable to determine the different loan amounts plus the interest paid.
26. Select F4 to G37.	
27. Select Data to Table....	The Table dialog box open.
28. Click the Column input cell: field.	You want to inform Excel that the table moves down a column, and the variable in the left column is a percentage (the same as D3).
29. Click cell D3.	See Figure 10.15.
30. Click OK.	Excel creates the table.
31. Select F5 to F37.	

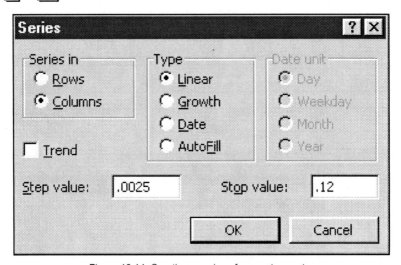

Figure 10.14: Creating a series of percentage rates

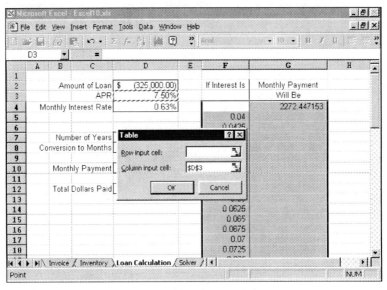

Figure 10.15: Defining the variable location

Step by Step	Additional Information
32. Click the `Percent Style` button.	**%** The Percent Style may be hidden in the Formatting Toolbar. The style is applied to the percentage series.
33. Click the `Increase Decimal` button.	**+.0 .00** The Increase Decimal may be hidden in the Formatting Toolbar. The display is corrected.
34. Select `G4` to `G37`.	
35. Click the `Currency Style` button.	**$** The Currency Style is found in the Formatting Toolbar. The display is corrected.
36. Click cell `D7`.	
37. Type **20** `Enter`.	The table updates, calculating results for a 20-year loan at different interest rates. See Figure 10.12.
38. Save your work.	
39. Leave this file open.	You will use it in the next exercise.

— User Notes—

Before You Begin Exercise D

Create a Two-Variable Data Table

Exercise Concepts

A two-variable data table uses two cells outside the table for comparison and reference. Two-variable data tables can answer more complex questions like "What if I save $1000.00 to $2000.00 per month for 72 to 144 months? How much would I save?" There are two variables that can change.

Creating a two-variable data table follows the same pattern as a one-variable data table. The exception is that the top row can contain a sample formula and a series of one of the variables. The other variable series is down the left side of the table. The upper-left corner of the table contains a formula-link to an area of comparison information.

Two-variable data tables also have two input cells. The comparison cell related to the top-row data series is the row-input cell. The comparison cell related to the column series in the table is the column-input cell.

Tips, Tricks, and Shortcuts

1. Do not change the values for either the row or column input cells. Doing so changes the formula in the upper-left corner but not in the table itself.

2. You can use the AutoFill feature or the Series command to create the two-variable data table's left column or top row.

3. To update the table, change a value in the comparison area, not in the table itself.

	A	B	C	D	E	F	G
			F14			=	500
13	STATE	CODE	TAX			72	
14	AK	5	0.07			500	
15	AL	6	0.065			650	
16	AR	5	0.05			800	
17	AZ	3	0.06			950	
18	CA	2	0.0725			1100	
19	CO	4	0.065			1250	
20	CT	7	0.07			1400	
21	DC	7	0.08			1550	
22	DE	7	0.07			1700	
23	FL	7	0.065			1850	
24	GA	7	0.06			2000	
25	HI	7	0.076			2150	
26	IA	4	0.06			2300	
27	ID	3	0.06			2450	
28	IL	4	0.08			2600	
29	IN	4	0.075			2750	
30	KS	4	0.0625			2900	

Invoice \ **Inventory** / Loan Calculation / Solver

Figure 10.16: Column series values

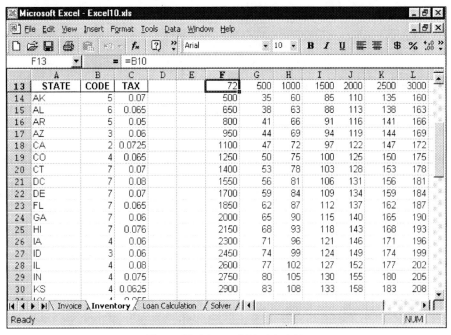

Figure .17: A two-variable data table

Exercise D: Create a Two-Variable Data Table

5
4
3
2
1

Level of
Difficulty

Step by Step	Additional Information

1. Make sure [Excel10.xls] is open.

2. Click the [Inventory] sheet tab.

   The Inventory worksheet becomes active. You will create a two-variable data table to calculate freight rates.

3. Scroll to and click cell [F13].

4. Type =**B10** [Enter].

5. Type **500** [Enter] **650** [Enter].

6. Select [F14] to [F15].

7. Drag the [AutoFill] handle to [F30].

   This column represents the value of the items shipped. See Figure 10.16.

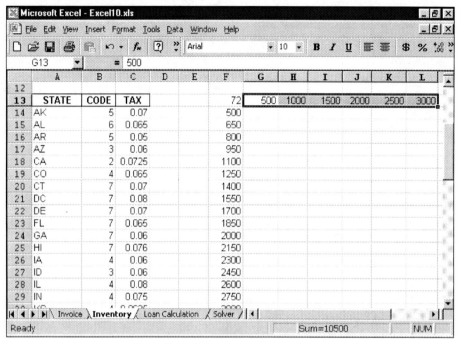

Figure 10.18: Column and row series values

Step by Step	Additional Information

8. Click cell G13.

9. Type **500** Tab **1000** Tab.

10. Select G13 to H13.

11. Drag the AutoFill handle to L13.   The row represents the shipping distance. See Figure 10.18.

12. Select F13 to L30.

13. Select Data to Table....   The Table dialog box opens. You must define two variable cells.

14. Click cell B8.   This defines the row input cell.

15. Click the Column input cell: field.

16. Click cell B9.   This defines the column input cell. See Figure 10.19.

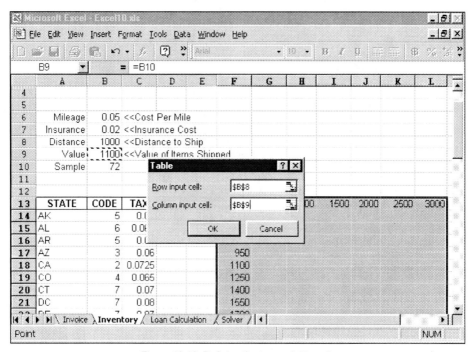

Figure 10.19: Defining the two variable cells

Step by Step	Additional Information
17. Click OK.	Excel calculates the freight rates based on the values found in the two variable cells.
18. Click cell F13.	The range is deselected.
19. Scroll to view the output.	See Figure 10.17.
20. Save your work.	
21. Leave this file open.	You will use it in the next exercise.

Before You Begin Exercise E

Use Solver

Exercise Concepts

To determine the total sales needed for the fourth quarter to reach the yearly goal, you would use Solver. Solver takes the formula in the target cell and adjusts the related changing cells and constraints to find the answer.

When using Solver, select the target cell to find the best value for the formula. Then select the changing cells that are related directly or indirectly to the formula in the target cell. The changing cells will adjust to meet the required goal in the target cell. Along with Solver, you can apply constraints [<=, =, >=, int (integer), bin (binary)] to restrict values in the changing cells.

Tips, Tricks, and Shortcuts

1. Press the Escape key to interrupt Solver.

2. Only apply Int (Integer) and Bin (Binary) in constraints to adjustable cells.

3. You must load Solver from the Add-Ins dialog box to work this exercise.

> To successfully complete this exercise, you must install the optional solver Add in. See the preface for installation notes.

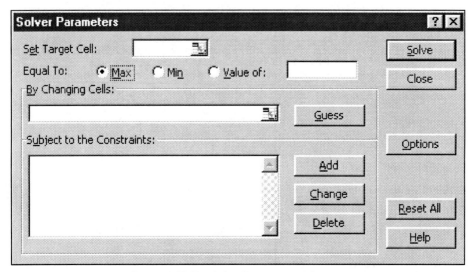

Figure 10.20: The Solver Parameters dialog box

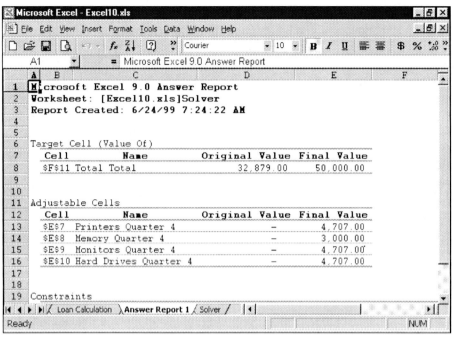

Figure .21: The Answer Report for Solver

Exercise E: Use Solver

Step by Step	Additional Information

1. Make sure Excel10.xls is open.

2. Click the Solver sheet tab.

3. Click cell E6.

   You will use solver to calculate how much earnings are needed in Quarter 4 to reach a total of $7,000.00.

4. Click the Tools to Add-Ins... check box.

5. Select Solver Add-in.

   Make sure there is a check mark in the check box.

6. Click OK.

   A dialog box informs you that this feature is not currently installed.

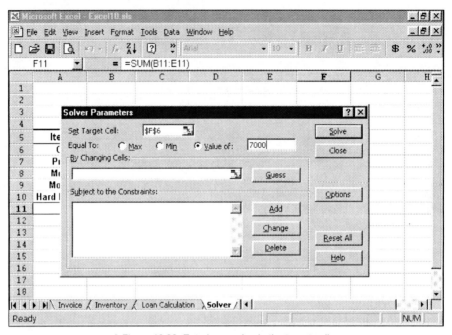

Figure 10.22: Entering a value in the target cell

Step by Step	Additional Information

7. Insert the installation CD-ROM in the drive and click Yes.

Excel loads the component from the installation CD-ROM. If the files are elsewhere, a dialog box will open. You can click the Browse button to navigate to the installation files.

8. Select Tools to Solver....

The Solver Parameters dialog box opens.

9. If necessary, click Reset All and then click OK.

You want to reset the dialog box. See Figure 10.20.

10. Click the Collapse Dialog button after Set Target Cell:.

The Solver Parameters dialog box minimizes and the worksheet displays.

11. Click cell F6.

Solver requires a formula in the target cell to work.

12. Press Enter.

The Solver Parameters dialog box reappears.

13. Select Value of: after Equal To:.

14. Press Tab.

The field after Value of: is selected.

Step by Step	Additional Information
15. Type **7000**.	See Figure 10.22.
16. Click the `Collapse Dialog` button after `By Changing Cells:`.	
17. Click cell `E6`.	Solver will change E6 to meet the required $7,000.00 total.
18. Press `Enter`.	
19. Click the `Solve` button.	The Solver Parameters dialog box closes and the Solver Results dialog box opens.
20. Make sure `Keep Solver Solution` is selected and press `Enter`.	The Solver Results dialog box closes and 1,855.00 displays as the total sales in Cables needed for Quarter 4.

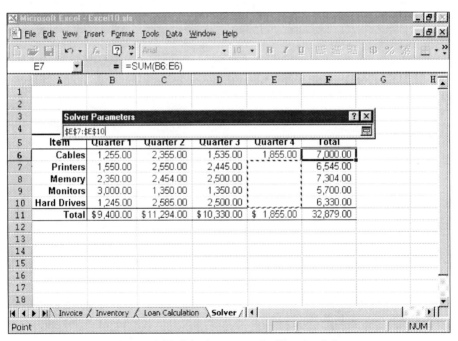

Figure 10.23: Selecting a range for Changing Cells

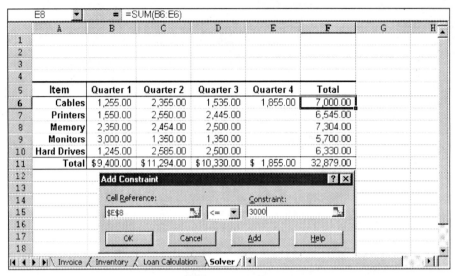

Figure 10.24: Adding a constraint to a value

Step by Step	Additional Information
21. Select ⌈Tools⌉ to ⌈Solver...⌉.	The Solver Parameters dialog box opens.
22. Click the ⌈Collapse Dialog⌉ button after ⌈Set Target Cell:⌉.	The Collapse Dialog box minimizes and the worksheet displays.
23. Click cell ⌈F11⌉.	Solver requires a formula in the target cell to work.
24. Press ⌈Enter⌉.	The Solver Parameters dialog box reappears.
25. Select ⌈Value of:⌉ after ⌈Equal To:⌉.	
26. Press ⌈Tab⌉.	The field after Value of: is selected.
27. Type **50000**.	
28. Click the ⌈Collapse Dialog⌉ button after ⌈By Changing Cells:⌉.	
29. Select cells ⌈E7⌉ to ⌈E10⌉.	Solver will change E7 to E10 to meet the required $50,000.00 total. See Figure 10.23.
30. Press ⌈Enter⌉.	
31. Click the ⌈Add⌉ button under ⌈Subject to the Contraints:⌉.	The Add Constraint dialog box opens.

M10–32

Step by Step	**Additional Information**

32. Click and drag the `Add Constraint` dialog box below the worksheet information.

33. Click the `Cell Reference:` field. — To make sure the cursor is in the field.

34. Click cell `E8`. — Cell E8 is added to the Cell Reference field.

35. Click the `Constraint:` field.

36. Type **3000**. — You want constraint the sales of Memory to 3000 for Quarter 4. See Figure 10.24.

37. Click the `Add` button.

38. Click cell `E10`.

39. Click the `Constraint:` field.

40. Type **7000**. — You want constraint the sales of Hard Drives to 7000 for Quarter 4.

41. Press `Enter`. — The Add Constraint dialog box closes and the Solver Parameters reappears.

42. Click the `Solve` button. — The Solve Parameters dialog box closes and the Solver Results dialog box opens.

43. Select `Answer` under `Reports`.

44. Click `OK`.

45. Click the `Answer Report 1` sheet tab. — See Figure 10.21.

46. Save your work.

47. Close the file.

48. Select `File` to `Exit`. — You have completed this module.

Module Review

True or False

1. If a series moves down a column, a one-variable data table should have a column input cell.

2. The top row of a one-variable data table can contain text, sample formulas, or a data series.

3. It is not necessary to include the left column labels in a VLOOKUP.

4. The HLOOKUP function searches a row for matching items.

5. A two-variable data table requires two variable cells, and both a row and column series to calculate variable results.

Multiple Choice

6. For an HLOOKUP to work properly, you must include:
   a. The top row of labels or values in the data table.
   b. The left column of labels or values in the data table.
   c. Both the top row and left column of labels and values.
   d. None of the above.

7. A two-variable data table must contain:
   a. A row input cell.
   b. A column input cell.
   c. Both row and column input cells.
   d. None of the above.

1. True; 2. False; 3. False; 4. True; 5. True; 6. a.; 7. c.

Study Guide

This study guide presents the skills mastered in this module. As a means of review, assess your comprehension for each skill.

Are you proficient in these skills?

Topic	Yes	Need Review
Use HLOOKUP	❏	❏
Use VLOOKUP	❏	❏
Create a One-Variable Data Table	❏	❏
Create a Two-Variable Data Table	❏	❏
Use Solver	❏	❏

To test your understanding of the concepts presented in this module, try the following:

Create a two-variable "what-if" data table for a home-mortgage business that includes a column of prices and a row of interest rates. Employ both the HLOOKUP and VLOOKUP functions to find and display the monthly payments for several different-priced homes at both 7% and 9% interest.

— User Notes —

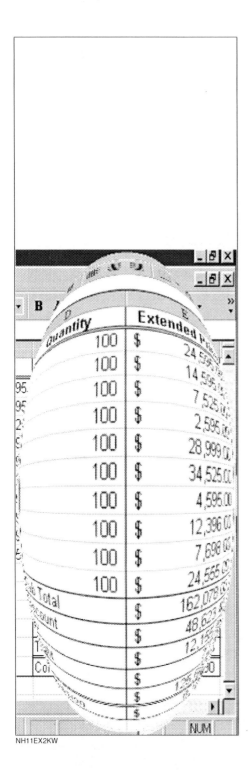

Advanced
Excel 2000 for Windows 95

MODULE

11

User- Defined Functions

Microsoft's powerful Visual Basic for Applications language allows you to create customized functions that perform a variety of useful tasks.

NH11EX2KW

— User Notes —

Module Preview: Function Procedures

You are probably well aware that Excel allows you to record commonly-used commands into macros. While you can record macros and play them back, you are limited to selecting commands in the menus and dialog boxes. You can, however, expand macro functionality and make a macro interactive by writing code that performs functions that are not in the basic command menus.

In this module, you will use Function Procedures. A function procedure contains Visual Basic statements enclosed by the *Function* and *End Function* statements. A Visual Basic statement is a complete syntax that shows an action, declaration, or definition.

When you write your macros, or function procedures, you bypass the recording process entirely. Since you are defining the function of the macro, these function procedures are known as user-defined functions.

Visual Basic, or VBA (Visual Basic for Applications), is not difficult to master, but you must learn and follow its rules. Proper syntax, grammar, and spelling are extremely important when writing Visual Basic code. If you violate any of the rules, the Visual Basic Editor starts debug mode and displays an error message. Although it is easy to correct mistakes, take the time to carefully write your code and you will encounter few problems.

You do not need to be a programmer to write function procedures in Visual Basic. You will gain an appreciation for the power and simplicity of this highly flexible language.

```
Public Function Discount(Sales, Customer)
    If Spacer = "R" Then
        Discount = Application.VLookup(Sales, Range("Discounts"), 2)
        GoTo Message
    ElseIf Customer = "W" Then
        Discount = Application.VLookup(Sales, Range("Discounts"), 3)
        GoTo Message
Message:    Discount = Discount * Sales
ElseIf Spacer = "" Then
    Discount = "Please Enter Customer Code"
Else
    Discount = "Invalid Customer Code"
```

Figure 11.1: Visual Basic code

— User Notes —

Module Objectives

Upon completion of this module,
you will master the skills necessary to:

A.   Create a Function Procedure

B.   Use an Application Object

C.   Control Procedure Flow

D.   Write a Subroutine

Before You Begin Exercise A

Create a Function Procedure

Exercise Concepts

To write a function procedure, you must write and store it in a Visual Basic module. You create a function procedure by combining mathematical expressions, existing functions, and Visual Basic code. Function procedures return a value based on the data provided, while recorded macros perform actions that alter cells, the worksheet, the workbook, etc.

Function procedures begin with *Function* and end with *End Function*. Recorded macros are subprocedures and are designated by the keywords *Sub* and *End Sub*. You can designate function procedure as either Public or Private.

The syntax of a function procedure consists of the name, arguments, code, expressions, and return value. Name your function procedure as you would a recorded macro. The arguments are the data that you provide and which enable the function to calculate a result. The code and expressions inform the function which calculations to perform. The return value is the result that you want displayed after the function completes the calculation.

Tips, Tricks, and Shortcuts

1. Enter the code carefully. If you make mistakes, the Visual Basic Editor displays an error message and attempts to debug the code.

2. If the error message, #NAME?, displays in a cell, Excel does not recognize your function procedure. Check to ensure that you gave your function procedure a name.

3. If the error message, #VALUE!, displays in a cell, you are specifying the incorrect arguments to the function procedure.

4. You can use either cell addresses or named ranges as arguments in a function procedure's code.

5. Select the Module option from the Insert menu to add a module.

6. Select the Procedure option from the Insert menu to open the Add Procedure dialog box. You can then name the procedure and specify its type and scope.

Figure 11.2: The Visual Basic Editor toolbar

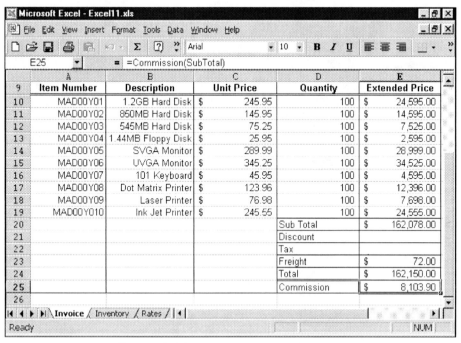

Figure 11.3: A function procedure returning a value

Exercise A: Create a Function Procedure

Level of
Difficulty

Step by Step	Additional Information
1. Make sure Excel 2000 is open.	
2. Close all open files.	
3. Select ⌐View⌐ to ⌐Toolbars⌐ to ⌐Customize...⌐.	The Customize dialog box opens.
4. Click the ⌐Options⌐ tab.	
5. Select ⌐Reset my usage data⌐ under ⌐Personalized Menus and Toolbars⌐.	To restore the default Toolbars.
6. Click ⌐Yes⌐.	

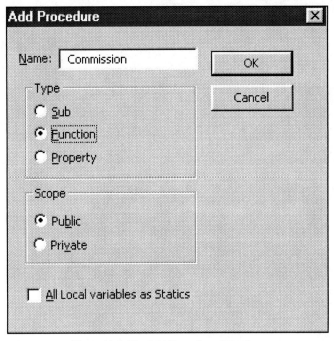

Figure 11.4: The Add Procedure dialog box

Step by Step	Additional Information
7. Click `Close`.	The Toolbars are restored.
8. Open `Excel11.xls`.	It is located in the Temp folder on the desktop.
9. Select `Tools` to `Macro` to `Visual Basic Editor`.	Or press Alt + F11. The Visual Basic Editor toolbar opens. See Figure 11.2.
10. If necessary, close the `Project` window.	
11. If necessary, close the `Properties` window.	
12. Select `Insert` to `Module`.	The Code window opens.
13. Click the `Maximize/Restore` button.	The Code window is maximized.
14. Select `Insert` to `Procedure...`.	The Add Procedure dialog box opens.

Step by Step	Additional Information
15. Type **Commission**.	To name the procedure.
16. Select Function under Type.	See Figure 11.4.
17. Click OK.	The code appears in the module.
18. Click between the () in Public Function Commission () .	The cursor is placed between the parentheses.
19. Type **SubTotal** Down Arrow.	This named range provides the argument necessary to perform the calculation.
20. Type **Commission=SubTotal*0.05** Down Arrow.	This calculates the commission rate. See Figure 11.5.
21. Click the View Microsoft Excel button.	The workbook file becomes active.
22. Scroll to and click cell E25.	

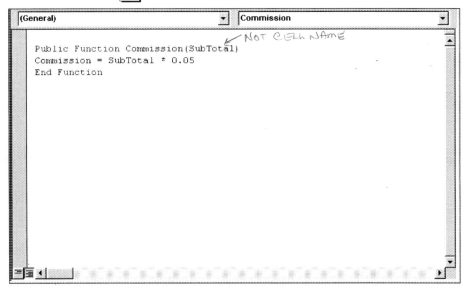

Figure 11.5: A function procedure

Step by Step	Additional Information
23. Type =`Commission(SubTotal)` `Enter` `Up Arrow`.	The user-defined function calculates a return value. See Figure 11.3.
24. Save your work.	
25. Remain in this screen.	You will use it in the next exercise.

— User Notes—

Before You Begin Exercise B

Use an Application Object

Exercise Concepts

If you require a more complex calculation or function, you can represent Excel's existing functions as application objects. An application object is a qualifier, which requests the program to use a specific setting, option, or worksheet function.

The syntax is the word *Application,* followed by the object name you want Excel to access, separated by a period. For example, you will write a function that locates a tax code in a data table and then calculates the total tax. Obviously, you need to employ the VLOOKUP function to locate the specific tax code in the table, and you, therefore, want the procedure to use the code representing that specific function: *Application.VLookup.*

Tips, Tricks, and Shortcuts

1. Enter the procedure code and data exactly as shown in the exercise steps to ensure that the procedure will perform the calculations correctly.

2. The correct syntax for any application object is *Application.object name.*

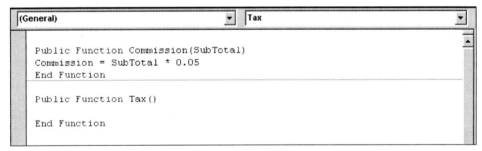

```
(General)                              ▼   Tax                              ▼

   Public Function Commission(SubTotal)
   Commission = SubTotal * 0.05
   End Function


   Public Function Tax()


   End Function
```

Figure 11.6: Adding a second function

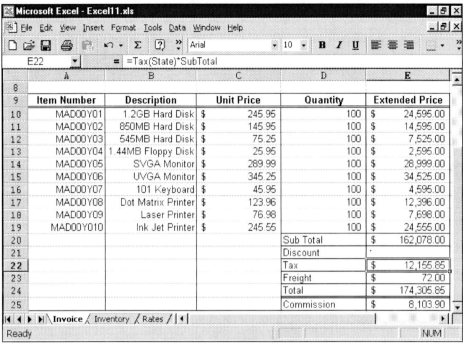

Figure 11.7: Calculating the total tax

Exercise B: Use an Application Object

Step by Step	Additional Information
1. Make sure Excel11.xls is open.	
2. Click the Microsoft Visual Basic button on the Taskbar.	The Visual Basic Editor becomes active.
3. Select Insert to Procedure....	The Add Procedure dialog box opens.
4. Type **Tax**.	To name the procedure.
5. Select Function under Type.	
6. Click OK.	The code appears in the module. A separator line divides the two functions. See Figure 11.6.
7. Click between the () after Public Function Tax.	The cursor is placed between the parentheses.

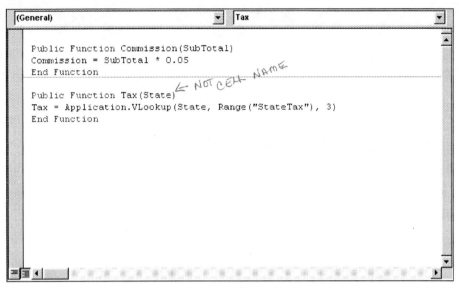

```
(General)                              ▼  Tax                              ▼

    Public Function Commission(SubTotal)
    Commission = SubTotal * 0.05
    End Function

    Public Function Tax(State)          ← NOT CELL NAME
    Tax = Application.VLookup(State, Range("StateTax"), 3)
    End Function
```

Figure 11.8: Using an application object

Step by Step	Additional Information

8. Type **State** Down Arrow.

9. Type **Tax=Application.Vlookup(State,Range("StateTax"),3)** Down Arrow.   See Figure 11.8.

10. Click the View Microsoft Excel button.   The workbook file becomes active.

11. Scroll to and click cell B6.

12. Type **CA** Enter.   To enter the state code in the comparison cell, so the VLookup application object can locate the correct tax.

13. Scroll to and click cell E22.

14. Type **=Tax(State)*SubTotal** Enter.   The user-defined function calculates the state tax.

Step by Step	Additional Information

15. Scroll to and click cell B6.

16. Type **NY** Enter.

17. Scroll to and click cell E22.

The user-defined function recalculated the state tax. See Figure 11.7.

18. Save your work.

19. Leave this file open.

You will use it in the next exercise.

Before You Begin Exercise C

Control Procedure Flow

Exercise Concepts

You can control the procedure flow of commands in a function procedure. For instance, you can insert a statement which instructs the function to stop or report errors encountered or make decisions based on specific criteria.

This decision-making process is accomplished through the use of logical testing. The *If, Then,* and *ElseIf* statements in the procedure control the actions of the function procedure based on encountered conditions. A specific line of code is executed based upon the outcome.

For example, perhaps you want to calculate different discount rates for wholesale and retail customers with each customer type represented by a special code. Depending on the entered code, the function decides which discount rate to use to calculate a result.

The syntax of this decision process is divided into three parts. There is the test: Which customer code is entered? If the function procedure finds one code, it executes one set of instructions. If it finds a different code, it executes an alternate set of instructions.

Tips, Tricks, and Shortcuts

All logical testing must begin with an *If* statement, contain an alternate *ElseIf* statement, and finish with an *EndIf.*

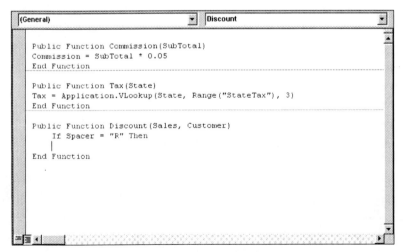

Figure 11.9: Entering an IF statement

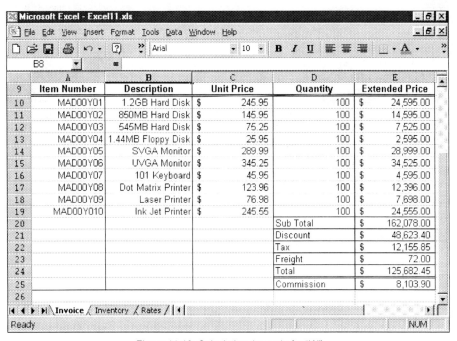

Figure 11.10: Calculating the code for "W"

Exercise C: Control Procedure Flow

5
4
3
2
1

Level of
Difficulty

Step by Step	Additional Information
1. Make sure `Excel11.xls` is open.	
2. Click the `Microsoft Visual Basic` button on the Taskbar.	The Visual Basic Editor becomes active.
3. Select `Insert` to `Procedure...`.	The Add Procedure dialog box opens.
4. Type **Discount**.	To name the procedure.
5. Select `Function` under `Type`.	
6. Click `OK`.	The code appears in the module.
7. Click between the `()` after `Public Function Discount`.	The cursor is placed between the parentheses.

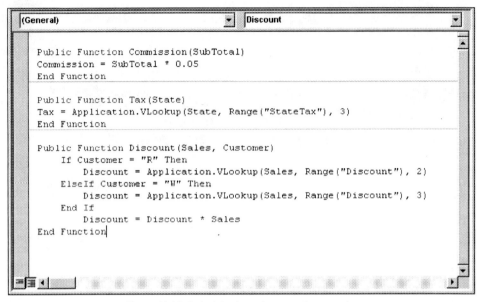

Figure 11.11: A decision based on a customer code

Step by Step	Additional Information

8. Type `Sales,Customer` Down Arrow .

9. Type Tab `If` Space `Customer="R"` Space `Then` Enter .

   This test determines the discount rate for an "R" or retail customer. See Figure 11.9.

10. Type Tab `Discount=Application.VLookup(Sales,Range("Discounts"),2)` Enter .

    If the test is true, then calculate the discount based on what is found in the data-table range named "Discounts" in the second column.

11. Type Backspace `ElseIf` Space `Customer="W"` Space `Then` Enter .

    However, determine the discount rate for a "W" or wholesale customer.

12. Type Tab `Discount=Application.VLookup(Sales,Range("Discounts"),3)` Enter .

    Calculate the discount based on what is found in the data-table range named "Discounts" in the third column.

13. Type Backspace `EndIf` Enter .

    This ends the testing.

Step by Step	Additional Information
14. Type `Tab` `Discount=Discount*` `Sales` `Down Arrow`.	See Figure 11.11.
15. Click the `View Microsoft Excel` button.	The workbook file becomes active.
16. Scroll to and click cell `B7`.	
17. Type `R` `Enter`.	To enter a customer code. See Figure 11.12.
18. Click cell `E21`.	
19. Type `=Discount(SubTotal,` `Customer)` `Enter`.	The function calculates the discount for an "R" or retail customer. What if the customer code is "W" or wholesale?
20. Click cell `B7`.	
21. Type `W` `Enter`.	
22. Click cell `E21`.	A new discount is calculated. See Figure 11.10.

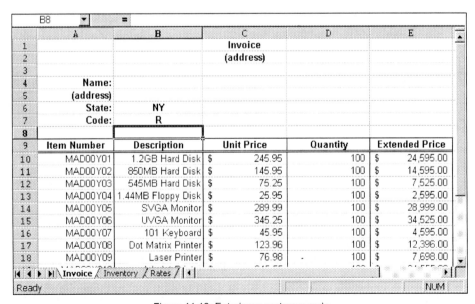

Figure 11.12: Entering a customer code

Step by Step	Additional Information
23. Save your work.	
24. Leave this file open.	You will use it in the next exercise.

— User Notes—

Before You Begin Exercise D

Write a Subroutine

Exercise Concepts

When you respond to a prompt or message from a user-defined function and enter data, you are working with an interactive procedure. If a novice user is working with Excel, it is more helpful to display prompts rather than confuse the user with error messages.

You can insert a subroutine (a program within a procedure) to display these messages, as opposed to writing another user-defined function. Simply add a *GoTo* statement to the procedure after performing a logical test to direct the control to the subroutine. The syntax is GoTo *line*; the *line* argument is either a label followed by a colon or a unique number. If you have a set of codes in a subroutine with *Message* as the line label, the command to route the control would be *GoTo Message*.

The code for the subroutine uses the same type of logical testing as the procedure itself. In the exercise, you will write a subroutine and alter the procedure to display messages based on the outcome of the tests.

Tips, Tricks, and Shortcuts

You can only branch to other lines using GoTo within a procedure. GoTo cannot branch to subroutines in other modules, workbooks, etc.

```
Public Function Discount(Sales, Customer)
    If Customer = "R" Then
        Discount = Application.VLookup(Sales, Range("Discounts"), 2)
        GoTo Message
    ElseIf Customer = "W" Then
        Discount = Application.VLookup(Sales, Range("Discounts"), 3)
    End If
        Discount = Discount * Sales

End Function
```

Figure 11.13: Inserted GoTo statement

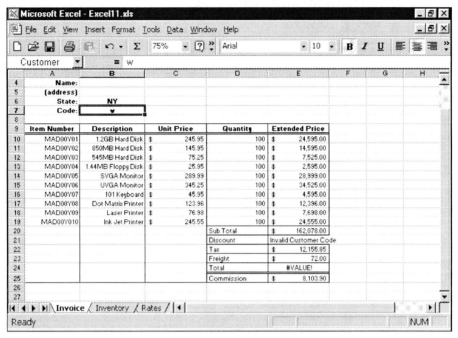

Figure 11.14: The subroutine displaying user prompts

Exercise D: Write a Subroutine

Step by Step	Additional Information

1. Make sure `Excel11.xls` is open.

2. Click the `Microsoft Visual Basic` button on the Taskbar.

   The Visual Basic Editor becomes active.

3. Click after `Discount=Application.VLookup...,2)`.

   You will modify the procedure code by adding a subroutine.

4. Press `Enter`.

   A new line is inserted.

5. Type **GoTo** `Space` **Message**.

   See Figure 11.13.

6. Click after `Discount=Application.VLookup...,3)`.

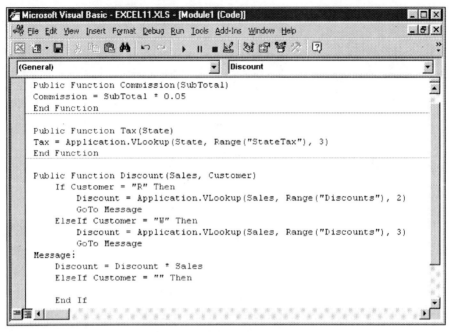

Figure 11.15: Testing for a missing entry

Step by Step   ## Additional Information

7. Press [Enter].

8. Type **GoTo** [Space] **Message** [Enter].   Now there are two GoTo Statements in the code.

9. Press [Backspace] twice.

10. Type **Message:** [Enter].

11. Type [Tab]
    Discount=Discount*Sales
    [Enter].

12. Type **ElseIf** [Space] **Customer="" **   This tests for a missing entry. See Figure 11.15.
    [Space] **Then** [Enter].

13. Type [Tab] **Discount="Please**   The subroutine displays this prompt if no entry
    Enter Customer Code" [Enter].   exists.

14. Press [Backspace].

Step by Step	Additional Information

15. Type **Else** `Enter`.

16. Type `Tab` **Discount="Invalid Customer Code"**.   Do not type the period.

17. Delete the `Discount=Discount*Sales` line beneath `EndIf`.   See Figure 11.16.

18. Click the `View Microsoft Excel` button.   The workbook file becomes active.

19. Click the `More Buttons` arrow on the Standard toolbar.

20. Click the `Zoom` arrow.   `100%` ▼ It is found within the Standard toolbar.

21. Select `75%`.   This reduces the view so you can view the results.

22. Click cell `B7`.

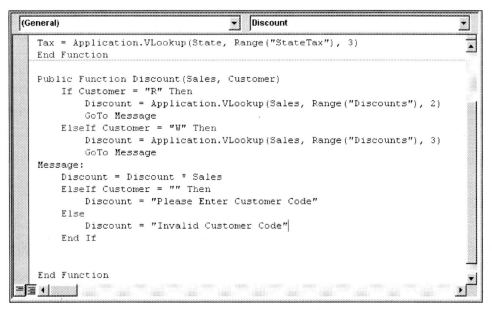

```
(General)                                    ▼   Discount                                        ▼

    Tax = Application.VLookup(State, Range("StateTax"), 3)
    End Function

    Public Function Discount(Sales, Customer)
        If Customer = "R" Then
            Discount = Application.VLookup(Sales, Range("Discounts"), 2)
            GoTo Message
        ElseIf Customer = "W" Then
            Discount = Application.VLookup(Sales, Range("Discounts"), 3)
            GoTo Message
    Message:
        Discount = Discount * Sales
        ElseIf Customer = "" Then
            Discount = "Please Enter Customer Code"
        Else
            Discount = "Invalid Customer Code"
        End If


    End Function
```

Figure 11.16: A subroutine added to a procedure

Step by Step	**Additional Information**
23. Press `Delete`.	The current code is erased. The message, "Please Enter Customer Code" displays in cell E21.
24. Type **w** `Enter` `Up Arrow`.	Type the "w" in lowercase only. The message, "Invalid Customer Code" displays. See Figure 11.14.
25. Type **W** `Enter`.	Type the "W" in uppercase only. A result displays in cell E21.
26. Save your work.	
27. Close the file.	You have completed this module.
28. Select `File` to `Exit`.	

Module Review

True or False

1. You can record function procedures.

2. A function procedure requires data from the user to return a value.

3. A function procedure can display a message.

4. A function procedure can be written directly on a worksheet.

5. Function procedures are capable of performing logical tests.

Multiple Choice

6. Function procedures begin and end with the keywords…

    a. Sub and End Function.

    b. Function and End Function.

    c. Sub and End Sub.

    d. Function and End Sub.

7. Which application object statement accesses the VLOOKUP function?

    a. App.VLookup

    b. VLookup.App

    c. Application.VLookup

    d. AppVLookup

1. False; 2. True; 3. True; 4. False; 5. True; 6. b.; 7. c.

Study Guide

This study guide presents the skills mastered in this module. As a means of review, assess your comprehension for each skill.

Are you proficient in these skills?

Topic	Yes	Need Review
Create a Function Procedure	❏	❏
Use an Application Object	❏	❏
Control Procedure Flow	❏	❏
Write a Subroutine	❏	❏

To test your understanding of the concepts presented in this module, try the following:

Create an invoice for your company. Create a user-defined function that prompts the user to enter the code for the address. Write a subroutine to test the contents of the address cell, stating that if the entry is lowercase, branch to a routine that displays a warning message which states that it must be entered in uppercase.

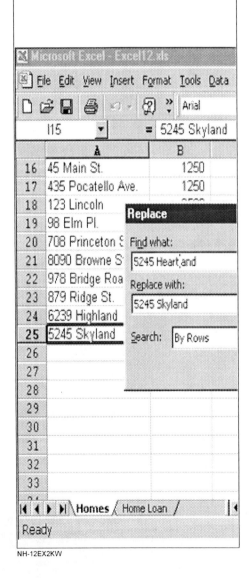

Advanced
Excel 2000 for Windows 95

MODULE

12

Customizing Excel

The powerful customization features in Excel allow you to simplify tasks and design efficient *environments*.

— User Notes —

Module Preview: Customizing Excel

The Excel interface is very flexible in creating custom menus, toolbars, and templates. The alteration of the interface reduces distractions and allows you to concentrate on specific tasks.

A custom menu allows you to group macros for easy access. You do not need to remember each macro's name, where they are stored, or the keystrokes to activate them. Instead, you can select them as you would any other menu option. You can arrange the menu option in any order and rename menu options.

Custom menus are not difficult to implement, but as with any kind of task, the best procedure is in stages. If you have a large library of macros, you have a good foundation on which to create your menu system. Assigning macros to your custom-menu options, or even the submenus, is easy but you should ensure that all the components operate correctly. You should test each macro thoroughly to ensure that the macro functions properly.

The custom toolbars are another way to improve the productivity of the environment. You can add specific buttons from various toolbars that you use most often to the custom toolbar. You can also add menu items and macros to the custom toolbar to further enhance your productivity.

Templates are another tool that can increase productivity. After you create a template that includes frequently-used styles, you can simply apply the template for consistent worksheet formatting.

This is the time to use all the techniques that you have learned to create a custom environment. Not only can you make your workspace more efficient, you can also simplify many complex tasks for other users.

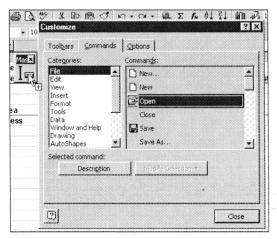

Figure 12.1: Creating a custom toolbar

— User Notes —

Module Objectives

Upon completion of this module,
you will master the skills necessary to:

A.   Create a Comment

B.   Create a Custom Menu

C.   Customize a Toolbar

D.   Work with Templates

Before You Begin Exercise A

Create a Comment

Exercise Concepts

As you create a worksheet, you become familiar with its contents and can navigate and alter it easily. However, a new user is unfamiliar with the functions associated with each cell. Consequently, you should document functions of important cells for the convenience of others who access the worksheet.

You can add Comments to alert users to the contents of a workbook. A Comment, which is designated by a small red triangle in the upper-right corner of a cell, is simply a message that is added to a cell location. Since it is not a part of the cell's content, it cannot be used in an Excel function. When a user moves the mouse pointer over a cell that contains a Comment, the note displays next to the cell.

Tips, Tricks, and Shortcuts

Select the Comment option from the Insert menu to create a Comment.

	A	B	C	D	E
1	**Address**	**Your Name:**		**Baths**	**Tub/Shower**
2	126 Florida St.	This workbook contains		1	Shower
3	129 Tornado St.	macros for navigating the		1.5	Shower
4	90 Lee Circle	database.		1	Tub
5	3092 Fairview Ave.			1.5	Shower
6	908 Logan Pl.	950	2	1.5	Shower
7	190 Alamo St.	950	2	1.5	Tub
8	50 Downing St.	950	2	2	Tub
9	23 Idaho St.	950	2	1.5	Shower
10	2353 Nebraska Ave.	950	2	1.5	Tub

Figure 12.2: Creating a Comment

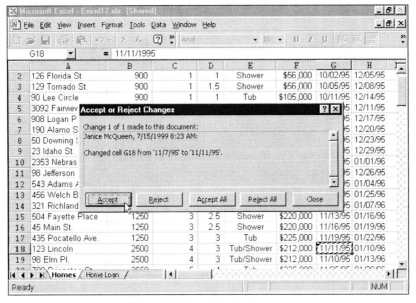

Figure 12.3: Accepting the changes

Exercise A: Create a Comment

| 5 |
| 4 |
| 3 |
| 2 |
| 1 |

Level of
Difficulty

Step by Step	Additional Information
1. Make sure Excel 2000 is open.	
2. Close all open files.	
3. Select [View] to [Toolbars] to [Customize...].	The Customize dialog box opens.
4. Click the [Options] tab.	
5. Select [Reset my usage data] under [Personalized Menus and Toolbars].	To restore the default Toolbars.
6. Click [Yes].	
7. Click [Close].	The Toolbars are restored.
8. Open [Excel12.xls].	Excel12.xls is located in the Temp folder on the desktop.
9. Click [Enable Macros].	You must enable the macros. The workbook opens.

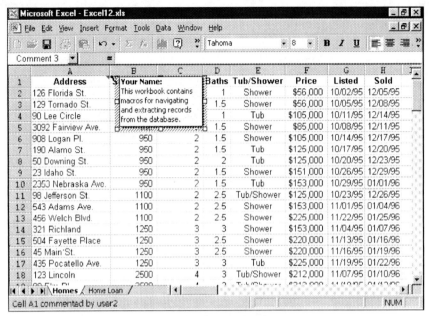

Figure 12.4: Editing a comment

Step by Step	Additional Information

10. Select Insert to Comment.

A comment box opens, and a red triangle displays in the upper-right corner of cell A1.

11. Type This workbook contains macros for navigating the database..

See Figure 12.2.

12. Click cell E1.

The comment box closes.

13. Move the pointer over cell A1.

The comment opens.

14. Right-click cell A1.

A shortcut menu opens.

15. Select Edit Comment.

You want to edit the comment.

16. Click after navigating.

17. Press the Spacebar.

18. Type and extracting records from.

See Figure 12.4.

M12–8

Step by Step	Additional Information

19. Click cell A1.

20. Select Edit to Clear to Comments.

21. Click cell A1. — See Figure 12.5. The red triangle disappears from cell A1.

22. Select Tools to Track Changes to Highlight Changes.... — The Highlight Changes dialog box opens.

23. Click Track changes while editing.... — Make sure there is a check mark in the check box.

24. Click the All arrow. — A list of options display.

25. Select Since I last saved. — See Figure 12.6.

26. Click OK three times.

27. Click cell A2.

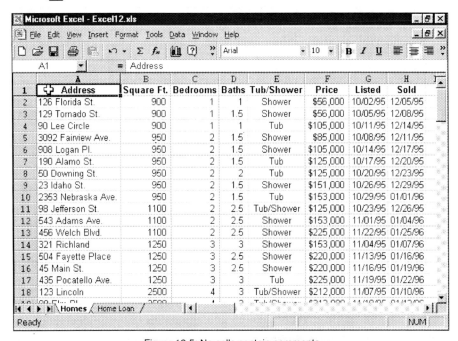

Figure 12.5: No cells contain comments

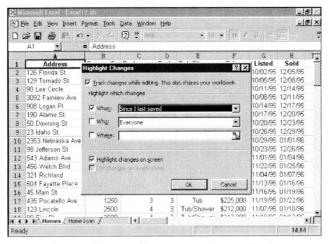

Figure 12.6: Tracking the changes for a workbook

Step by Step	Additional Information
28. Type 123 Florida Ave. Enter.	The cell is highlighted to show it has been changed.
29. Place the cursor over cell A2.	Do not click. A comment displays showing the changes.
30. Select Tools to Track Changes to Accept or Reject Changes....	
31. Click OK.	The Select Changes to Accept or Reject.
32. Click the Not yet reviewed arrow.	
33. Select Since date....	
34. Click OK.	The Accept or Reject Changes dialog box opens.
35. Click Reject.	The Accept or Reject Changes dialog box closes and the text is restored to its original state.
36. Scroll to row 18 and select 11/07/95.	
37. Type 11/11/95 Enter.	
38. Select Tools to Track Changes to Accept or Reject Changes....	
39. Click OK.	The Select Changes to Accept or Reject.

Step by Step	Additional Information

40. Click the `Not yet reviewed` arrow.

41. Select `Since date...`.

42. Click `OK`. | The Accept or Reject Changes dialog box opens.

43. Click `Accept`. | The Accept or Reject Changes dialog box closes and the new text is accepted. See Figure 12.3.

44. Save your work.

45. Leave this file open. | You will use it in the next exercise.

Before You Begin Exercise B

Create a Custom Menu

Exercise Concepts

Excel allows you to create custom menus and menu items which you can position anywhere on the menu bar. When you open the Customize dialog box, you start a design mode that applies to the entire user interface.

Creating a custom menu is as simple as selecting a category, selecting a command, and dragging the command to a position on the menu bar. When you move either a menu or menu item into position, an I-beam displays as a visual reference. This horizontal or vertical I-beam indicates the exact position of the menu or menu item when you release the mouse button.

Right-clicking the new menu or menu item displays shortcuts. You can select the default text in the Name box and replace it your own text. If you place an ampersand (&) before a specific letter in the item's title, the following letter will be underlined. This gives you the option of using keystrokes to start the new item's macro. Be careful where you place the ampersand since you cannot use any of the underlined letters that distinguish the remaining menu items.

Tips, Tricks, and Shortcuts

1. Select the Customize option from the Tools menu to open the Customize dialog box.

2. The Categories and Commands lists are in the Commands section of the Customize dialog box.

3. The horizontal or vertical I-beam indicates the position of the menu or menu item when the mouse button is released.

4. You can move default menus to any position on the menu bar while the Customize dialog box is open.

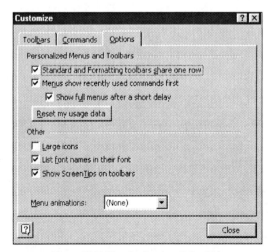

Figure 12.7: The Customize dialog box

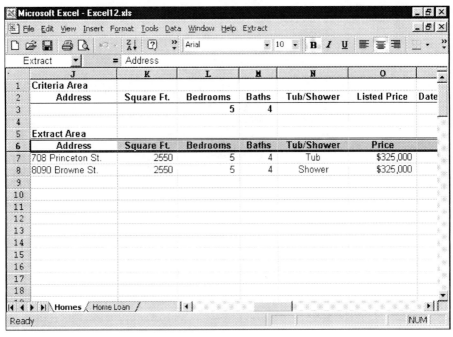

Figure 12.8: Using the custom menu

Exercise B: Create a Custom Menu

5
4
3
2
1

Level of
Difficulty

Step by Step	Additional Information
1. Make sure `Excel12.xls` is open.	
2. Scroll to and click cell `L3`.	
3. Type 4 `Tab` 3 `Enter`.	This enters criteria for the query.
4. Select `Tools` to `Customize...`.	The Customize dialog box opens. See Figure 12.7.
5. Click the `Commands` tab.	The dialog box updates.
6. Scroll to and select `New Menu` under `Categories:`.	
7. Click and hold `New Menu` under `Commands:`.	The cursor becomes a moving pointer.

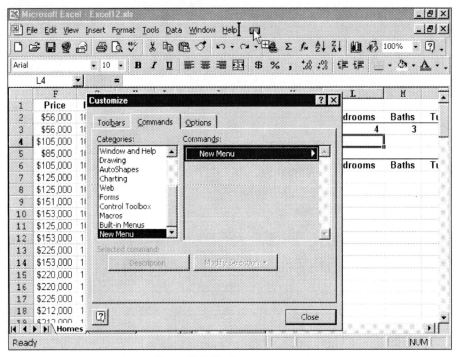

Figure 12.9: Placing a new menu

Step by Step	Additional Information
8. Drag up and to the right of `Help` on the menu bar.	An I-beam displays to the right of the Help menu. See Figure 12.9.
9. Release the mouse button.	The New Menu item is placed on the menu bar.
10. Right-click `New Menu` on the menu bar.	A shortcut menu opens.
11. Select `New Menu` in the `Name:` box.	Click and drag to highlight the text.
12. Type **E&xtract** `Enter`.	The new name replaces the default text. The "x" in Extract is underlined.
13. Select `Macros` under `Categories:`.	The dialog box updates.
14. Click and hold `Custom Menu Item` under `Commands:`.	
15. Drag up and hold over `Extract`.	A gray square appears below the menu.

M12–14

Step by Step	Additional Information
16. Drag the pointer over the gray square.	The I-beam appears on the square. See Figure 12.10.
17. Release the mouse button.	The Custom Menu Item appears below the Extract menu.
18. Right-click `Custom Menu Item`.	A shortcut menu opens.
19. Select `&Custom Menu Item` in the `Name:` box.	Click and drag to select the text.
20. Type &New.	The new name replaces the default text.
21. Select `Assign Macro...`.	The Assign Macro dialog box opens.
22. Select `NewEntry` under `Macro name:`.	See Figure 12.11.
23. Click `OK`.	The Customize dialog box reappears.

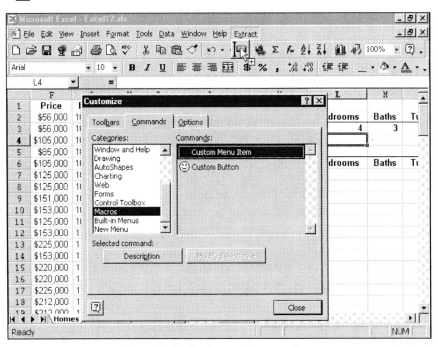

Figure 12.10: Placing a custom menu item

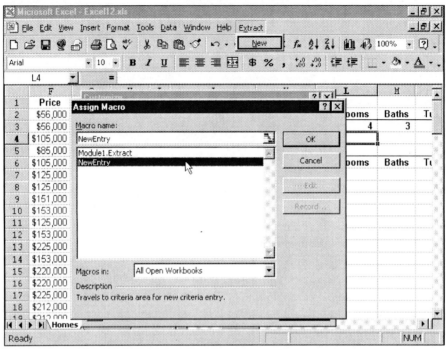

Figure 12.11: Assigning a macro to a custom menu item

Step by Step	Additional Information
24. Click and hold `Custom Menu Item` under `Commands:`.	
25. Drag up and hold over `Extract`.	The New menu item displays.
26. Drag down and hold just below `New`.	The I-beam appears beneath the New menu item text.
27. Release the mouse button.	The Custom Menu Item appears below the New menu item.
28. Right-click `Custom Menu Item` under `New`.	A shortcut menu opens.
29. Select `&Custom Menu Item` in the `Name:` box.	Click and drag to select the text.
30. Type `&Perform`.	The new name replaces the default text.

M12–16

Step by Step	Additional Information
31. Select `Assign Macro...`.	The Assign Macro dialog box opens.
32. Select `Module1.Extract` under `Macro Name:`.	
33. Click `OK`.	
34. Click `Close`.	The Customize dialog box closes.
35. Select `Extract` to `Perform`.	The options on the Extract menu are linked to the macros. Records are extracted from the database. See Figure 12.12.
36. Select `Extract` to `New`.	The cell selector moves into the criteria range.
37. Click cell `L3`.	
38. Type 5 `Tab` 4 `Enter`.	

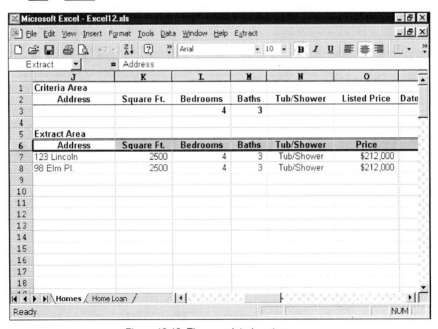

Figure 12.12: The completed custom menu

Step by Step	Additional Information
39. Select Extract to Perform.	The records matching the criteria are extracted. See Figure 12.8.
40. Save your work.	
41. Leave this file open.	You will use it in the next exercise.

— User Notes—

Before You Begin Exercise C

Customize a Toolbar

Exercise Concepts

You can create custom toolbars and use them in any open workbook. The toolbars can contain default or custom buttons.

You can create a new toolbar in the Toolbars section of the Customize dialog box. You must enter a name for the custom toolbar before you access the Commands section. The custom toolbar, which is wide enough for one tool face or button, appears on top of the active worksheet. Drag and drop the buttons onto the custom toolbar from any of the existing command categories, and the custom toolbar will expand to accommodate the additional buttons.

A custom toolbar has the characteristics of any default toolbar. A ToolTip will appear when you move the pointer to a button. You can also right-click to open the Toolbar shortcut menu.

Tips, Tricks, and Shortcuts

1. You can drag any button or menu to a new position on the custom toolbar while the Customize dialog box is open.

2. To use Subtotals, sort the labeled columns, A to Z or Z to A, and select Subtotals. Choose the options you desire to subtotal each category separately by row.

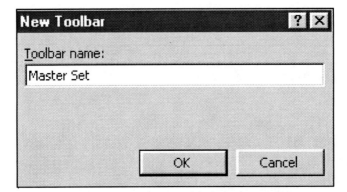

Figure 12.13: Naming the custom toolbar

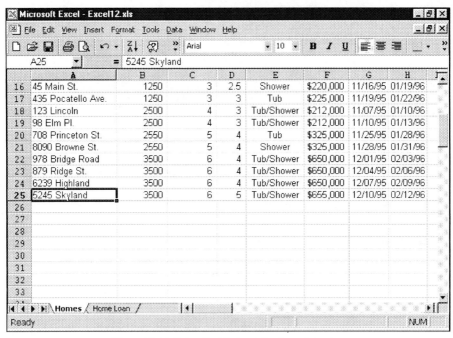

Figure 12.14: Using the Find and Replace dialog box

Exercise C: Customize a Toolbar

Step by Step	Additional Information

1. Make sure Excel12.xls is open.

2. Select Tools to Customize... .   The Customize dialog box opens.

3. If necessary, click the Toolbars tab.   The dialog box updates.

4. Click New... .   The New Toolbar dialog box opens.

5. Type **Master Set**.   See Figure 12.13.

6. Click OK .   The new toolbar appears.

7. Click the Commands tab.   The dialog box updates.

8. Select File under Categories: .

Level of Difficulty

5
4
3
2
1

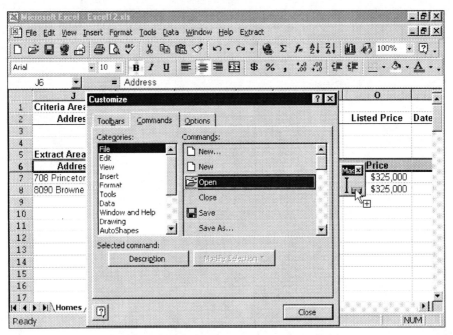

Figure 12.15: Positioning a button on the toolbar

Step by Step	Additional Information

9. Click and hold the Open button under Commands:.

10. Drag the Open button onto the new toolbar. See Figure 12.15.

11. Click and hold the Save button under Commands:.

12. Drag the Save button onto the new toolbar. To the right of the Open button.

13. Scroll to and select Charting under Categories:. A new set of commands displays.

14. Scroll to and select Chart Wizard under Commands:.

Step by Step	Additional Information

15. Drag the Chart Wizard button onto the new toolbar. To the right of the Save button

16. Click and hold Extract on the menu bar.

17. Drag the menu to the new toolbar. To the right of the Chart/Wizard button   The custom menu is placed on the toolbar.

18. Click Close.   The Customize dialog box closes. See Figure 12.16.

19. Select View to Toolbars to Master Set.   The Master Set toolbar closes.

20. Right-click the Worksheet Menu bar.   A shortcut menu opens.

21. Select Master Set.   The Master Set toolbar reappears.

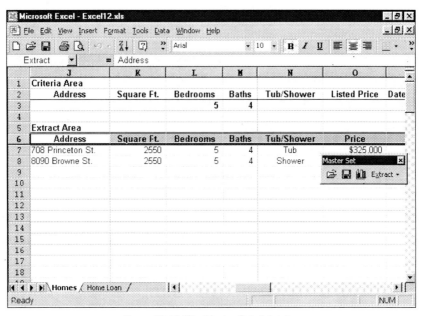

Figure 12.16: The Master Set dialog box

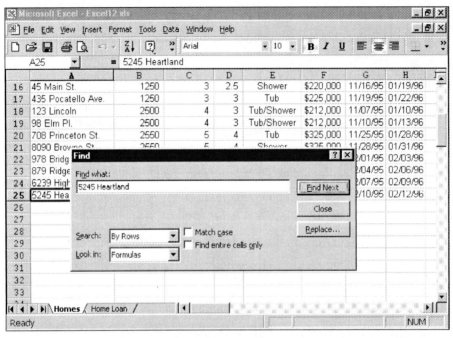

Figure 12.17: The Find dialog box

Step by Step	Additional Information
22. Select View to Toolbars to Customize....	The Customize dialog box opens.
23. Click the Toolbars tab.	
24. Scroll down and double-click Master Set under Toolbars:.	To remove the check mark from the check box. The Master Set toolbar closes.
25. Click Close.	The Customize toolbar dialog box closes.
26. Press Control + Home.	You return to cell A1.
27. Select Edit to Find....	The Find dialog box opens.
28. Type 5245 Heartland.	
29. Click Find Next.	5245 Heartland is found in the database. See Figure 12.17.

Step by Step	Additional Information
30. Click Replace....	The Replace dialog box updates and Replace with: displays.
31. Type 5245 Skyland	You want to replace Heartland with Skyland in the database.
32. Click Replace.	
33. Click Close.	See Figure 12.14.
34. Save your work.	
35. Leave this file open.	You will use it in the next exercise.

Before You Begin Exercise D

Work with Templates

Exercise Concepts

Templates are time savers that allow you to create new documents quickly and easily. An Excel template is a master document that enables you to create other Excel documents that look and behave like the template.

You can create your own customized template or use a template that's included with Excel. For example, if you bill customers on a regular basis, you can create an invoice template. When it is time to bill customers, you simple insert an invoice template that includes the appropriate formatting and performs the appropriate calculations. You will save time and invoices will have a consistent appearance.

Tips, Tricks, and Shortcuts

1. To view an Excel template, click the Spreadsheet Solutions tab within the New dialog box.

2. Select a template to view its contents in the preview window.

3. When saving a template, Excel automatically changes the directory to the template folder in C:\Windows\Application Data\Microsoft\Templates.

4. To view a template, click the General tab within the New dialog box.

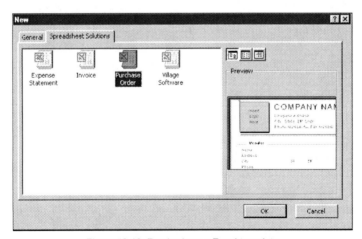

Figure 12.18: Previewing an Excel template

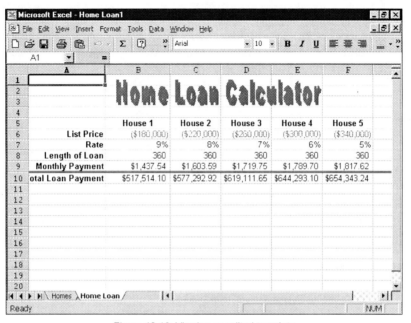

Figure 12.19: Viewing an edited template

Exercise D: Work with Templates

5
4
3
2
1

Level of
Difficulty

Step by Step	Additional Information
1. Make sure Excel12.xls is open.	
2. Click the Home Loan sheet tab.	
3. Select File to New... .	The New dialog box opens.
4. Click the Spreadsheet Solutions tab.	
5. Click the Purchase Order icon.	The Purchase Order template displays in the Preview window. See Figure 12.18.
6. Click OK .	
7. Click the Enable Macros button.	
8. Click the Close Window button.	To close the Purchase Order Template.
9. Click No .	You do not want to save the template. The Excel12.xls spreadsheet reappears.

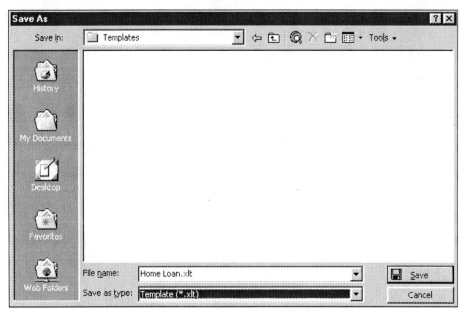

Figure 12.20: Saving a workbooks as a template

Step by Step	Additional Information
10. Select cells B5 to C10.	
11. Drag the autofill handle to cell F10.	
12. Click cell A1.	
13. Select File to Save As....	The Save As dialog box opens.
14. Type Home Loan after File name:.	To name the template.
15. Click the arrow after Save as type:.	A list of different file types displays.
16. Select Template (*.xlt).	The Template extension is added to the file name and the Templates folder is selected after the Save in field. See Figure 12.20.
17. Click Save.	
18. Click the Close Window button.	Home Loan.xlt closes.
19. Select File to New....	The New dialog box opens.

Step by Step	Additional Information
20. Click the General tab.	
21. Click Home Loan.xlt.	Notice that the Home Loan.xls template displays in the Preview window. See Figure 12.21.
22. Click OK.	
23. Click Enable Macros.	A copy of the Home Loan Calculator template displays.
24. Click the Close Window button.	Home Loan.xlt closes.
25. Select File to Open....	The Open dialog box opens.
26. Open Home Loan.xlt.	The path is C:\Windows\Application Data\Microsoft\Templates\Home Loan.xlt.
27. Click Enable Macros.	
28. Select cells A6 to A10 and B5 to F5.	To format the text.
29. Click the Bold button.	The text becomes bold.

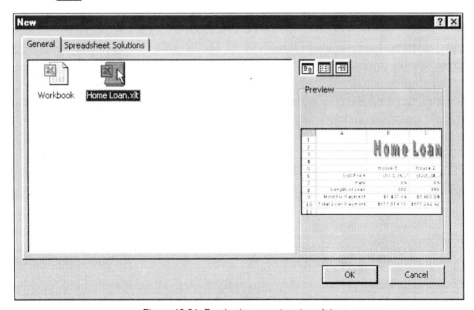

Figure 12.21: Previewing a custom template

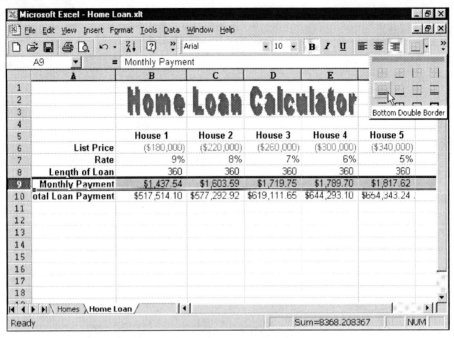

Figure 12.22: Adding a border to the template

Step by Step

Additional Information

30. Click the row ⑨ row header.

31. Click the `More Buttons` arrow on the Formatting toolbar.

32. Click the `Borders` arrow.

33. Select `Bottom Double Border`.

A border is added to the template. See Figure 12.22.

34. Click cell `A1`..

35. Click the `Save` button.

36. Click the `Close Window` button.

37. Select `File` to `New...`.

38. Double-click `Home Loan.xlt`.

© New Horizons Publishing Center

Step by Step	Additional Information
39. Click Enable Macros.	The Home Loan template displays the newly formatted template. See Figure 12.19.
40. Select cell B10 to F10.	
41. Select Format to Cells....	The Format Cells dialog box opens.
42. Click the Number tab.	
43. Select Accounting under Category:.	
44. Click the down arrow twice after Decimal places:.	The Decimal place is zero.
45. Click OK.	
46. Select Format to Cells....	The Format Cells dialog box opens.
47. Click the Number tab.	
48. Select Number under Category:.	
49. Click the up arrow twice after Decimal places:.	The Decimal place is zero.
50. Click OK.	
51. Select cells B10 to F10.	
52. Select Format to Cells....	The Format Cells dialog box opens.
53. Select Custom under Category:.	
54. Select the field under Type:.	
55. Type #,#.00 Enter.	The Numbers change according to the custom format you specified.
56. Select File to Exit.	You do not need to save. You have completed this module.

Module Review

True or False

1. Custom menus and items cannot be accessed using keystrokes.

2. While the Customize dialog box is open, you can move default menus to any position on the menu bar.

3. Custom toolbars do not have the characteristics of default toolbars.

4. The default folder for a custom template is the Templates folder.

5. Custom tools have no commands or macros assigned to them.

Multiple Choice

6. The character used to denote an underlined menu letter is…
    a. *.
    b. $.
    c. &.
    d. #.

7. Which extension is the correct extension for an Excel Template?
    a. .xls
    b. .xlt
    c. .xlw
    d. .tmp

1. False; 2. True; 3. False; 4. True; 5. True; 6. c.; 7. b.

Study Guide

This study guide presents the skills mastered in this module. As a means of review, assess your comprehension for each skill.

Are you proficient in these skills?

Topic	Yes	Need Review
Create a Comment	❑	❑
Create a Custom Menu	❑	❑
Customize a Toolbar	❑	❑
Work with Templates	❑	❑

To test your understanding of the concepts presented in this module, try the following:

Create a user-defined menu system that incorporates the use of macros presently in a workbook file. Insert a new menu and menu items between the Data and Window menus. Modify the startup defaults so that Excel automatically opens a specific workbook document.

— User Notes—

Advanced Excel 2000 for Windows 95 Post-test

Directions: Circle the correct answers

Module 9

1. An IF function formula has three arguments: the test, an "if true" statement, and an "if false" statement. (TRUE – FALSE)
2. IF functions can be nested within one another. (TRUE – FALSE)
3. The AND logical function tests multiple conditions, of which any can be true. (TRUE – FALSE)
4. IF functions cannot display text strings; they can only calculate results. (TRUE – FALSE)
5. The NOT logical function returns the reverse value for the condition tested. (TRUE – FALSE)
6. Goal Seek finds a solution by...
   a. changing the formula cell.
   b. adjusting the value in a single cell.
   c. adjusting the values in multiple cells.
   d. none of the above
7. The correct syntax for the AND function in an IF logical formula is
   a. =AND(IF(B2>10000,B8>4),B2*B4,B2*E4)
   b. =AND(=IF(B2>10000,B8>4),B2*B4,B2*E4)
   c. =IF(AND(B2>10000,B8>4),B2*B4,B2*E4)
   d. =(IF/AND((B2>10000,B8>4),B2*B4,B2*E4))

Module 10

1. If a series moves down a column, a one-variable data table should have a column input cell. (TRUE – FALSE)
2. The top row of a one-variable data table can contain text, sample formulas, or a data series. (TRUE – FALSE)
3. It is not necessary to include the left column labels in a VLOOKUP. (TRUE – FALSE)
4. The HLOOKUP function searches a row for matching items. (TRUE – FALSE)
5. A two-variable data table requires two variable cells, and both a row and column series to calculate variable results. (TRUE – FALSE)
6. For an HLOOKUP to work properly, you must include:
   a. The top row of labels or values in the data table.
   b. The left column of labels or values in the data table.
   c. Both the top row and left column of labels and values
   d. None of the above.
7. A two-variable data table must contain:
   a. A row input cell.
   b. A column input cell.
   c. Both row and column input cells.
   d. none of the above

Module 11

1. You can record function procedures. (TRUE – FALSE)
2. A function procedure requires data from the user to return a value. (TRUE – FALSE)
3. A function procedure can display a message. (TRUE – FALSE)
4. A function procedure can be written directly on a worksheet. (TRUE – FALSE)
5. Function procedures are capable of performing logical tests. (TRUE – FALSE)
6. Function procedures begin and end with the keywords...
   a. Sub and End Function.
   b. Function and End Function.
   c. Sub and End Sub.
   d. Function and End Sub.
7. Which application object statement accesses the VLOOKUP function?
   a. App.VLookup
   b. VLookup.App
   c. Application.VLookup
   d. AppVLookup

Module 12

1. Custom menus and items cannot be accessed using keystrokes. (TRUE – FALSE)
2. While the Customize dialog box is open, you can move default menus to any position on the menu bar. (TRUE – FALSE)
3. Custom toolbars do not have the characteristics of default toolbars. (TRUE – FALSE)
4. The default folder for a custom template is the Templates folder. (TRUE – FALSE)
5. Custom tools have no commands or macros assigned to them. (TRUE – FALSE)
6. The character used to denote an underlined menu letter is...
   a. *.
   b. $.
   c. &.
   d. #.
7. Which extension is the correct extension for an Excel Template?
   a. .xls
   b. .xlt
   c. .xlw
   d. .tmp

Answer Key

Module 9: 1. T, 2. T, 3. F, 4. F, 5. T, 6. b., 7. c.

Module 10: 1. T, 2. T, 3. F, 4. T, 5. F, 6. a., 7. c.

Module 11: 1. F, 2. T, 3. T, 4. F, 5. T, 6. b., 7. c.

Module 12: 1. F, 2. T, 3. T, 4. T, 5. F, 6. c., 7. b.

New Horizons Computer Learning Centers
Return on Investment for Computer Training

The following questions allow you to calculate your return on investment in computer training, and see how much you benefit when you choose New Horizons for your computer training.

What are your annual salary, taxes,
and benefits?   Salary $_____ X 120%............ (a) $ _____
This model assumes taxes and benefits are equal to 20%. If your taxes and benefits are not 20%, adjust the percentage above.

What percentage of your job involves using
this program?.. (b) _____ %

The cost to operate this program is .... (c) $ _____
Multiply (a) times (b).

What was your score on the Post-test? .... (d) _____ %
Percentage of correct answers.

What was your score on the Pre-test? .... (e) _____ %
Percentage of correct answers.

Your percentage improvement in operating this
program is.. (f) _____ %
Subtract (e) from (d) and divide the result by (e).

The Financial Return for taking this class is .... (g) $ _____
Multiply (c) times (f).

How much did you pay for this class? .... (h) $ _____

Your daily rate including benefits .... (i) $ _____
Divide (a) by 240 working days.

The total cost for you attending the class .... (j) $ _____
Add (h) and (i).

Your **Return on Investment** for this class is .... (k) _____ %
Divide (g) by (j).

Excel 2000
for Windows 95

APPENDICES

Quick Reference Guide

File

New	=	`Control` + `N`
Open	=	`Control` + `O`
Save	=	`Control` + `S`
Print	=	`Control` + `P`

Edit

Undo	=	`Control` + `Z`
Repeat	=	`Control` + `Y`
Cut	=	`Control` + `X`
Copy	=	`Control` + `C`
Paste	=	`Control` + `V`
Fill Down	=	`Control` + `D`
Fill Right	=	`Control` + `R`
Clear Contents	=	`Delete`
Find	=	`Control` + `F`
Replace	=	`Control` + `H`
Go To	=	`Control` + `G`

Format

Format Cells	=	`Control` + `1`
Bold	=	`Control` + `B`
Italic	=	`Control` + `I`
Underline	=	`Control` + `U`
Strikeout	=	`Control` + `S`
Apply #,##0.00 Number Format	=	`Control` + `Shift` + `!`
Apply $#,##0.00 Number Format	=	`Control` + `Shift` + `$`
Apply 0% Number Format	=	`Control` + `Shift` + `%`

Tools

Spelling	=	`F7`
Macros	=	`Alt` + `F8`
Visual Basic Editor	=	`Alt` + `F11`

Help

Office Assistant	=	`F1`
What's This?	=	`Shift` + `F1`

Function Shortcut Keys

Insert new worksheet	=	`Alt` + `Shift` + `F1`
Insert a chart sheet	=	`Alt` + `F1`
Save As	=	`Alt` + `F2`
Edit active cell	=	`F2`
Edit cell comment	=	`Shift` + `F2`
Save	=	`Alt` + `Shift` + `F2`
Paste Name	=	`F3`
Paste Function	=	`Shift` + `F3`
Define Name	=	`Control` + `F3`
Create names from labels	=	`Control` + `Shift` + `F3`
Redo/Repeat last action	=	`F4`
Repeat Find or Go To	=	`Shift` + `F4`
Close active window	=	`Control` + `F4`
Exit program	=	`Alt` + `F4`
Go To	=	`F5`
Find	=	`Shift` + `F5`
Restore window	=	`Control` + `F5`
Next window	=	`F6`
Previous pane or workbook	=	`Shift` + `F6`
Next workbook window	=	`Control` + `F6`
Spelling	=	`F7`

Function Shortcut Keys (continued)

Move window	=	[Control] + [F7]
Extend cell selection	=	[F8]
Add to the selection	=	[Shift] + [F8]
Resize the window	=	[Control] + [F8]
Macros	=	[Alt] + [F8]
Calculate workbook	=	[F9]
Calculate active worksheet	=	[Shift] + [F9]
Minimize workbook	=	[Control] + [F9]
Activate menus	=	[F10]
Display shortcut menu	=	[Shift] + [F10]
Maximize/Restore document window	=	[Control] + [F10]
Chart	=	[F11]
Insert a new worksheet	=	[Shift] + [F11]
Insert Excel 4.0 Macro Sheet	=	[Control] + [F11]
Visual Basic Editor	=	[Alt] + [F11]
Save As	=	[F12]
Save	=	[Shift] + [F12]
Open	=	[Control] + [F12]
Print	=	[Control] + [Shift] + [F12]

Worksheet Direction Keys - Ready Mode

One cell left	=	`Left Arrow` or `Shift` + `Tab`
One cell right	=	`Right Arrow` or `Tab`
One cell up	=	`Up Arrow`
One cell down	=	`Down Arrow`
Cell A1 of active worksheet	=	`Control` + `Home`
Previous page	=	`Page Up`
Next page	=	`Page Down`
Move to first cell in column A	=	`Home`
Move right to last active cell	=	`End` + `Right Arrow`
Move left to last active cell	=	`End` + `Left Arrow`
Move up to last active cell	=	`End` + `Up Arrow`
Move down to last active cell	=	`End` + `Down Arrow`

Area

Left one character	=	`Left Arrow`
Right one character	=	`Right Arrow`
Enter data and move up one cell	=	`Up Arrow`
Enter data and move down one cell	=	`Down Arrow` or `Enter`
Erase one character to left of cursor	=	`Backspace`
Move to the preceding word	=	`Control` + `Left Arrow`
Move to the following word	=	`Control` + `Right Arrow`
Move cursor to end of line	=	`End`
Places entry into active cell	=	`Enter`
Erases entry in Edit mode	=	`Escape`

Key	Function	SHIFT	CTRL	CTRL+SHIFT	ALT	ALT+SHIFT
F1	Get Help. Displays the Assistant balloon if the Assistant is turned on	Select the options you want. For help on an option, select the option, and press Shirt + F1			Create a chart that uses the current range	Insert a new worksheet
F2	Edit the active cell and position the insertion point at the end of the line	Edit a cell comment			Save the active workbook	Display the Save as dialog box
F3	Paste a defined name into a formula	Paste a function into a formula	Define a name	Create names from row and column labels		
F4	Repeat the last action	Repeat the last Find action (same as Find Next)	Close the active workbook window			
F5	Display the Go To dialog box	Display the Find dialog box	Restore the active workbook window size			
F6	Move to the next pave in a workbook that has been split	Move to the previous pane in a workbook that has been split	Move to the next workbook or window	Move to the previous workbook or window		
F7	Display the Spelling dialog box		Carry out the Move command (workbook icon menu, menu bar), or use the arrow keys to move the window			
F8	Turn on extending a selection by using the arrow keys	Add another range of cells to the selection; or use the arrow keys to move to the start of the range you want to add, and then press F8 and the arrow keys to select the next range	Carry out the Size command (workbook), or use the arrow keys to size the window		Display the Macro dialog box	
F9	Calculated all sheets in all open workbooks	Calculate the active worksheet	Minimize the workbook window to an icon			
F10	To make the menu bar active, or close a visible menu and submenu at the same time	Show a shortcut menu	Maximize or restore the workbook window			
F11	Create a chart that uses the current range	Insert a new worksheet	Insert a Microsoft Excel 4.0 macro sheet		Display the Visual Basic Editor	
F12	Save the active workbook	Display the Save as dialog box	Display the Open dialog box	Display the Print dialog box		

Glossary of Terms

Absolute Reference
A cell address or range name that always refers to the same location in a formula's arguments even if the formula is copied or moved. Adding dollar signs before the formula arguments designates an absolute reference. See *Arguments* and *Relative Referencing*.

Active Cell
The cell displayed with a heavy border; it indicates that the cell is selected.

Address
The location of a particular cell in a workbook, identified by the worksheet name, column letter, and row number. See *Cell Address*.

Arguments
The cell addresses that contain the data necessary for a formula to calculate a result, such as, cell addresses, text, and numeric data.

Auditing
The process of analyzing a spreadsheet for errors and determining the relationships between cells and formulas in a worksheet.

AutoCalculate
A feature that allows you to check the result of a selected range of cells containing numerical information before entering an actual formula. The default functions include Average, Count, Count Nums, Max, Min, and Sum.

AutoComplete
A feature that tracks the data entries made by a user into a worksheet, and automatically completes them.

AutoCorrect
A feature that automatically corrects common spelling and formatting errors as you enter data into a worksheet.

AutoFill
A feature that allows you to add data using the fill handle located in the active cell border. This feature recognizes date, time, text, and trend data.

AutoFilter
A feature that allows you to specify criteria to instantly view subsets of data contained within a database.

AutoFormat
A feature that allows you to apply a predefined format to a range of worksheet data.

AutoSum
A feature that allows you to quickly sum rows and columns of numerical entries.

Cell
The intersection of a column and row. It is the smallest unit of a worksheet. You can enter and store data as text, values, functions, or formulas.

Cell Address
The address of the column and row intersection that forms a cell. For example, the intersection of column B and row 4 designates the cell address as B4.

Chart
A visual depiction of selected worksheet data. The ranges selected and plotted against each other are known as data series.

Chart Objects
The individual graphic elements of a chart. These objects can be manipulated to create special graphic presentation effects.

Chart Sheet
One of the three document types available in Excel. A chart sheet is used to store any charts created by a user. See *Chart*.

Chart Wizard
A special feature that guides a user through the creation and annotation of the graphic objects in a chart.

Circular Reference
A condition that occurs when the cell address containing a formula is included in the arguments of the formula itself. See *Relative Referencing* and *Absolute Reference*.

Column Headers

The heading box at the top of each worksheet column. The headers are labeled A through IV. See *Row Headers*.

Conditional Formatting

A format, such as, cell shading or font color, that Excel automatically applies to cells if a specified condition is true.

Criteria

The conditions specified during a query to filter records from a database.

Criteria Range

The defined range containing the field names necessary for selecting records.

Data Form

A feature that allows for the editing, addition, and deletion of records from a database.

Data Map

A special OLE program designed to create geographical maps from data in a worksheet.

Data Series

A range of data used to create a chart.

Data Table

A special table in which a series of variables are substituted in the formulas to predict different outcomes.

Database

A collection of related items that are organized into records and classified by named fields. The fields are contained in worksheet columns and records are placed in worksheet rows.

Field

A database cell belonging to the category designated by its field name.

Field Names

The names that represent a specific column of data in a database worksheet. A field name can be thought of as the category of items in the database.

Footers

Information that appears along the bottom edge of a printed page of worksheet output, such as, titles, names, page numbers, etc.

Formatting

The application of specific attributes to the contents of a worksheet. These attributes control the final appearance of the worksheet. They may include character and numerical formatting.

Formula

An equation that calculates a result and displays it in the worksheet.

Formula Bar

The portion of the Excel window that is used to enter or edit data or formulas in a worksheet cell. It also displays the constant value or formula contained in the active cell.

Function

A prefabricated Excel formula designed to return a value based on a range of cells. An example of a function is the =SUM function. The argument (the data supplied by the user) is the range of cells to be added.

Function Macro

A macro that contains formulas or other calculations.

Function Palette

A special feature that guides you through the creation and editing of complex formulas.

Goal Seek

A feature that "backward solves" problems by changing values in variable cells, thus forcing the formula dependent on those values to calculate a desired result.

Headers

Information that appears along the top edge of a printed page of worksheet output, such as, titles, names, page numbers, etc.

Label

The text heading in a cell that describes the row or column of values.

Linking Formula

A formula containing an external cell reference to another worksheet or workbook. It is used to link separate worksheets or workbooks by using a special syntax to reference cells that contain data to calculate results.

Macro
A collection of instructions and worksheet commands that automatically perform one or more tasks. Macros are created to save time and customize the user interface.

Marquee
A moving outline of dots surrounding a selected range of cells.

Menu Bar
The bar at the top of the Excel window that displays the names of the menus.

Module
One of three document types available in Excel. A module stores macro commands recorded or created by the user to accomplish a specific task. See *Macro*.

Named Cells
Also known as Named Ranges. Excel allows a user to assign a unique name to a cell or group of cells.

Operators
The symbols that express the relationship between items known as operands. These symbols commonly include the plus sign (+), minus sign(-), the asterisk (*)for multiplication, and the forward slash (/) for division.

Panes
A display option that is used to simultaneously display several open workbooks. Selecting the Split command from the Window menu creates panes.

Range
A rectangular group of contiguous selected cells.

Record
A collection of information about a particular item. An Excel database is divided into records. Each record is further divided into fields. A record is placed in a row in the database. All records in a database have the same number of fields, even though some may not contain data.

Relative Referencing
The relative adjustment of cell addresses in a formula when the formula is copied or moved in the worksheet. Opposite of *Absolute Reference*.

Row Header
The heading box at the left of each worksheet row. The headers are numbered 1 through 65536. See *Column Header*.

Scenario Manager
A feature that allows you to track changes in sets of data.

Shortcut Menu
A menu that opens when you right-click an object. If you right-click a portion of the worksheet, the standard shortcut menu opens. If you right-click a toolbar, a special toolbar shortcut menu opens.

Status Bar
The bar along the bottom of the Excel program window that displays the current command functions, the next step, or a definition of the current activity.

Template
A specialized Excel worksheet or workbook that can contain predefined formulas, formatting, text, and macros, and can be fully customized by the user.

Value
A numerical entry in a worksheet cell.

Workbook
The basic Excel document that consists of a collection of worksheets.

Worksheet
One of the three document types available in Excel. The worksheet is similar to a large columnar pad that is divided into rows and columns. The intersection of a column and row forms a cell. Cells are used to store and manipulate data. See *Module* and *Chart Sheet*.

The Windows

The Excel 2000 Window

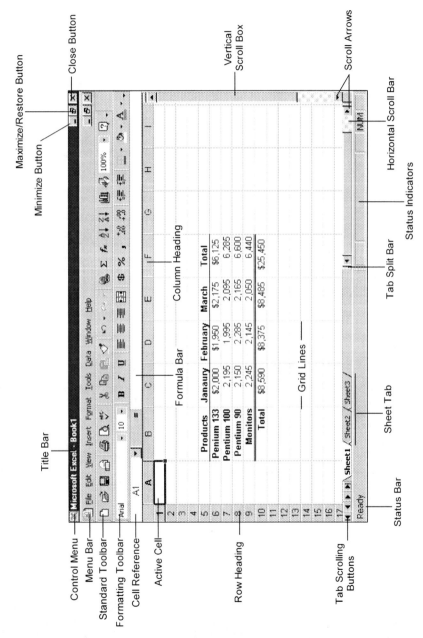

Close Button

Maximize/Restore Button

Minimize Button

Vertical Scroll Box

Scroll Arrows

Horizontal Scroll Bar

Status Indicators

Tab Split Bar

Column Heading

Formula Bar

Grid Lines

Sheet Tab

Title Bar

Control Menu

Menu Bar

Standard Toolbar

Formatting Toolbar

Cell Reference

Active Cell

Row Heading

Tab Scrolling Buttons

Status Bar

Products	Janaury	February	March	Total
Penium 133	$2,000	$1,950	$2,175	$6,125
Pentium 100	2,195	1,995	2,095	6,285
Pentium 90	2,150	2,285	2,165	6,600
Monitors	2,245	2,145	2,050	6,440
Total	$8,590	$8,375	$8,485	$25,450

The Visual Basic Window

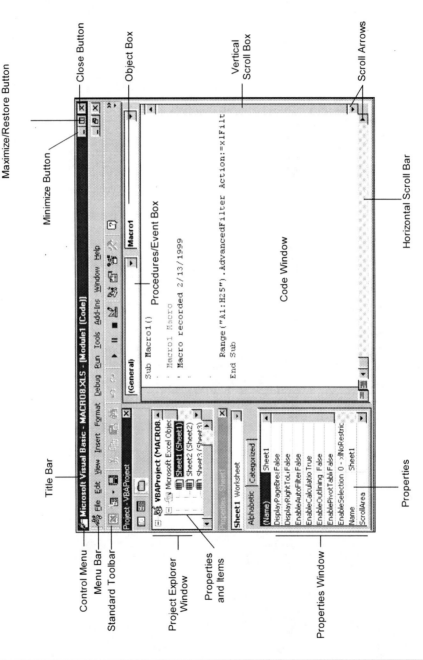

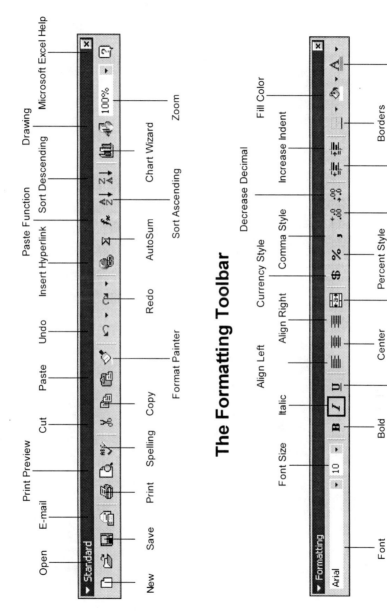

The Standard Toolbar

New · Open · E-mail · Print Preview · Cut · Paste · Undo · Insert Hyperlink · Paste Function · Sort Descending · Drawing · Microsoft Excel Help

Save · Print · Spelling · Copy · Format Painter · Redo · AutoSum · Sort Ascending · Chart Wizard · Zoom

The Formatting Toolbar

Font · Font Size · Italic · Underline · Align Left · Align Right · Currency Style · Comma Style · Decrease Decimal · Increase Indent · Fill Color · Font Color

Bold · Center · Merge and Center · Percent Style · Increase Decimal · Decrease Indent · Borders

The Drawing Toolbar

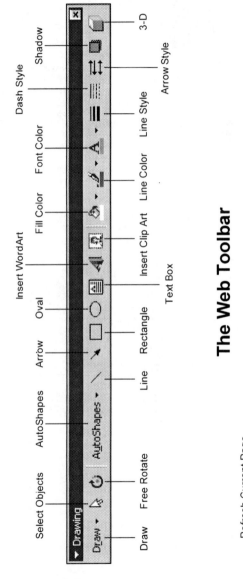

Select Objects — AutoShapes — Insert WordArt — Fill Color — Font Color — Dash Style — Shadow — 3-D

Draw — Free Rotate — Line — Arrow — Oval — Rectangle — Text Box — Insert Clip Art — Line Color — Line Style — Arrow Style

The Web Toolbar

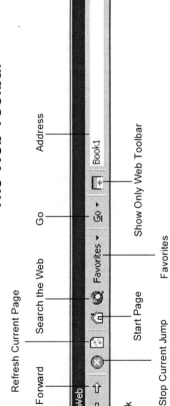

Refresh Current Page — Search the Web — Go — Address — Show Only Web Toolbar

Forward — Back — Stop Current Jump — Start Page — Favorites

The Toolbars
The 3-D Setting Toolbar

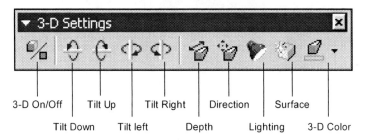

The Auditing Toolbar

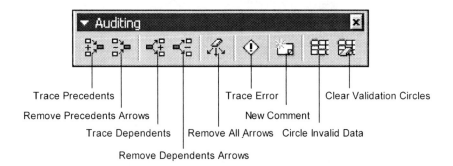

The Chart Toolbar

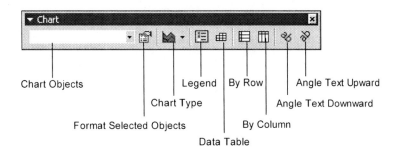

The Shadow Settings Toolbar

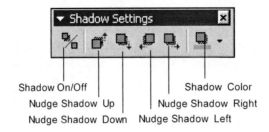

Shadow On/Off

Nudge Shadow Up

Nudge Shadow Down

Shadow Color

Nudge Shadow Right

Nudge Shadow Left

The Visual Basic Toolbar

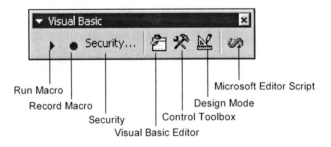

Run Macro

Record Macro

Security

Visual Basic Editor

Microsoft Editor Script

Design Mode

Control Toolbox

The WordArt Toolbar

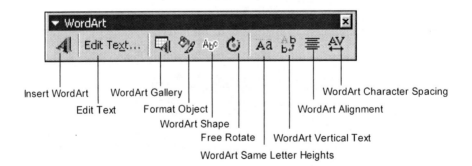

Insert WordArt

Edit Text

WordArt Gallery

Format Object

WordArt Shape

Free Rotate

WordArt Same Letter Heights

WordArt Character Spacing

WordArt Alignment

WordArt Vertical Text

The External Data Toolbar

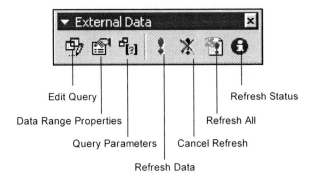

Edit Query

Data Range Properties

Query Parameters

Refresh Data

Refresh Status

Refresh All

Cancel Refresh

The Picture Toolbar

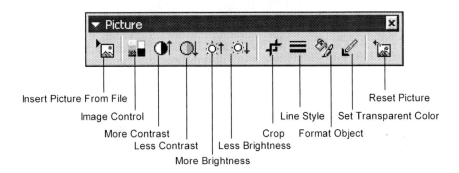

Insert Picture From File

Image Control

More Contrast

Less Contrast

More Brightness

Less Brightness

Crop

Line Style

Format Object

Set Transparent Color

Reset Picture

The Full Screen Toolbar

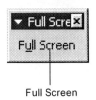

Full Screen

The Circular reference Toolbar

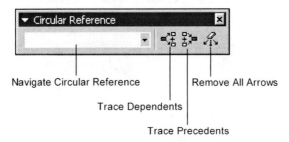

Navigate Circular Reference

Trace Dependents

Trace Precedents

Remove All Arrows

The Clipboard Toolbar

Paste All

Clear Clipboard

Copy

Toolbar

Empty

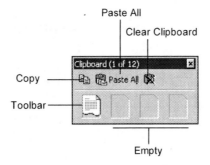

The Exit Design Mode Toolbar

Design Mode

The PivotTable Toolbar

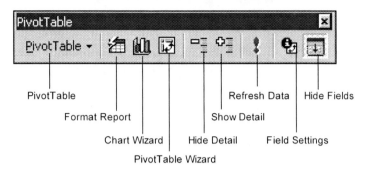

PivotTable

Format Report

Chart Wizard

PivotTable Wizard

Refresh Data   Hide Fields

Show Detail

Hide Detail   Field Settings

The Reviewing Toolbar

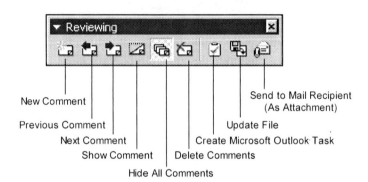

New Comment

Previous Comment

Next Comment

Show Comment

Hide All Comments

Send to Mail Recipient
(As Attachment)

Update File

Create Microsoft Outlook Task

Delete Comments

The Stop Recording Toolbar

Record Macro ——— ● ——— Relative Reference

The Control Toolbox Toolbar

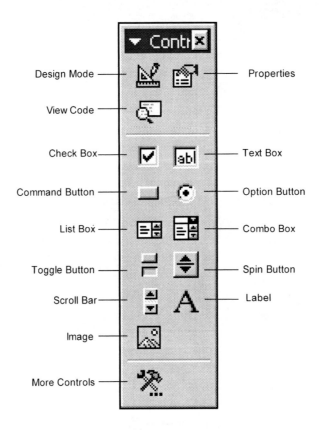

Design Mode ——— Properties

View Code ———

Check Box——— ——— Text Box

Command Button ——— ——— Option Button

List Box ——— ——— Combo Box

Toggle Button ——— ——— Spin Button

Scroll Bar——— ——— Label

Image ———

More Controls ———

The Forms Toolbar

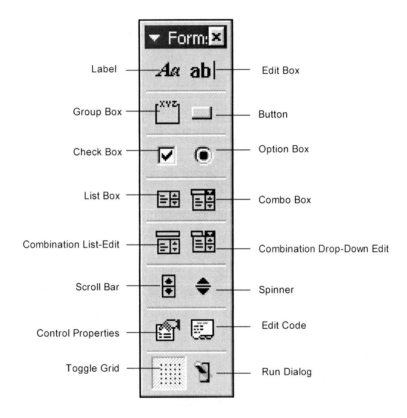

Label — Edit Box

Group Box — Button

Check Box — Option Box

List Box — Combo Box

Combination List-Edit — Combination Drop-Down Edit

Scroll Bar — Spinner

Control Properties — Edit Code

Toggle Grid — Run Dialog

The Menus

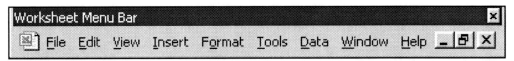

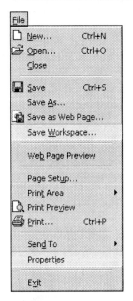

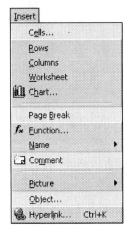

The Menus

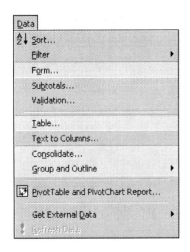

The Menus

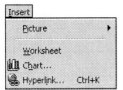

The Menus

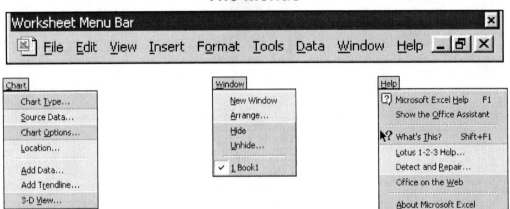

Using the Mouse

The Interface With a Tail

Moving the Mouse

The mouse is a computer interface. You use it to tell the computer what you want to do. How? It uses a roller ball to transfer the movement of the mouse on the desktop to the cursor on the screen. There are little rollers in the mouse that the roller ball moves against. There is one that rolls up and down, and one that rolls right and left.

The cursor has several different shapes depending on the application you are using. Three common cursor shapes you will use frequently are the pointer, the I-beam cursor, and the crosshair pointer. The pointer shape has a hot spot at the tip of the arrow. You will use the hot spot at the tip of the arrow when pointing and clicking on icons or objects. The I-beam is for entering text and most resembles the flashing cursor on DOS-based programs. And the crosshair is for drawing and graphics.

Pointing and Clicking

The mouse for Windows may have two or three buttons. Generally, the right mouse button is used only for specific program functions, although the mouse can be switched so that the right mouse button becomes the main button you use in an application. Unless otherwise stated, in the text, a click of the mouse will refer to a click of the left mouse button.

Clicking and Dragging

Objects such as icons, folders, and graphics can be moved by clicking and dragging the mouse. To move an icon, for example, click on the icon without releasing the mouse button. Drag the pointer to the new location you desire. The icon will move along under the pointer as you drag. When you release the mouse button the icon will be dropped. It is much like moving paper clips with a magnet.

Shift-Clicking

Shift-clicking enables you to select multiple objects. When you wish to select objects in a Windows program, you can click on an object and while holding the shift key, select other objects, all of which will become selected. You can also deselect one of a group of selected items by holding the Shift key when you click on the item you want to deselect.

Pointer Marquee

A similar group selection feature that is available in many programs that run under Windows is called the pointer marquee. Using this feature, you can click and drag to surround one or more items to be included in a selected group. It is important to know that the cursor must be away from the items you wish to select prior to making your marquee.

As a pointing tool the mouse is used to select items on the screen. When you point on the item you want to select, click the button once. This will select the item that you are pointing to. If the item is an icon, it will turn dark indicating that it has been selected. If you point and click on another icon the selected icon will return to normal. It has been deselected. When a new item is selected, the previous item automatically deselects.

Double-clicking

To double-click, press the mouse button rapidly twice. It might take some practice to get the feel of this since different mice have different *feels* to them. Double-clicking can launch an application, close an active window; open a directory, or select a word.

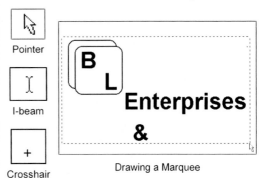

Pointer

I-beam

Crosshair

Drawing a Marquee

The Enhanced Keyboard (101)

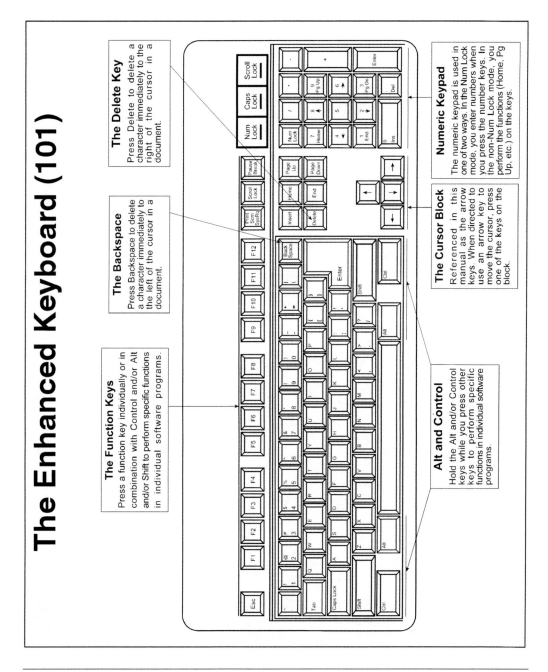

The Delete Key
Press Delete to delete a character immediately to the right of the cursor in a document.

The Backspace
Press Backspace to delete a character immediately to the left of the cursor in a document.

The Function Keys
Press a function key individually or in combination with Control and/or Alt and/or Shift to perform specific functions in individual software programs.

Numeric Keypad
The numeric keypad is used in one of two ways. In the Num Lock mode, you enter numbers when you press the number keys. In the non-Num Lock mode, you perform the functions (Home, Pg Up, etc.) on the keys.

The Cursor Block
Referenced in this manual as the arrow keys. When directed to use an arrow key to move the cursor, press one of the keys on the block.

Alt and Control
Hold the Alt and/or Control keys while you press other keys to perform specific functions in individual software programs.

Index

The Index of New Horizons User Manuals provides quick access to information by subject. Normally the topics are cross–referenced to popular third party manuals published by Que or Sybex. Neither of those manuals was available at press time.

Topics are listed in the first column. The second column references the module and page number for each topic in the New Horizons manual.